In his book *ReClaimed Church*, D
path for seeing churches revitalize
gives insight as to why churches beg...
to ReClaim them. His wisdom is not from a merely academic position,
rather from the heart of a man who has learned these lessons through the
day-to-day trenches of real ministry. If your church is declining and in
desperate need of revitalization, this book is a must read!

Dr. Nathan Lorick, executive director
Colorado Baptist General Convention

Church revitalization is one of the most pressing issues in American evan-
gelicalism today. Bill Henard's *ReClaimed Church* provides both insight-
ful analysis of dying churches and practical steps to revitalizing them,
all drawn from biblical principles. Developed and refined from teaching
churches, seminaries, and associations, *ReClaimed Church* provides a
wealth of sound instruction and solid examples making it indispensable
to pastors seeking church revitalization.

Thom S. Rainer, president and CEO
LifeWay Christian Resources

I was delighted when I heard Dr. Henard was writing this book. Why?
Because many North American churches are in need of change. Because
good resources on revitalization are few in light of massive needs. Because
Henard knows the Word, leadership, strategy, and change. Because Henard
loves Jesus and His Church so much he is willing to say the things most of
us do not want to hear. This book was forged from years of experience and
research. Ponder these words for your context and apply accordingly.

J. D. Payne, PhD, pastor of church multiplication
The Church at Brook Hills

Understanding how churches grow, decline, and are revitalized is essential
for all who love and lead the church. Dr. Henard writes with the mind
of a scholar, the heart of a shepherd, and the skills of a practitioner. This
book provides a valuable contribution to God's kingdom work.

Seth Polk, lead pastor
Cross Lanes Baptist Church
Cross Lanes, West Virginia

ReClaimed Church is a good contribution to the field of church revitalization. Dr. Henard utilizes recent research to great effect. He thoroughly discusses topics such as life stages of churches, types of revitalization, and church conflict. His book is practical; for example, he explains why some common messages on church signs ("Come Grow with Us" and "All Welcome") may not send the message that is intended. He also provides an interesting discussion concerning a covenant of revitalization. I heartily recommend this book.

Mike Morris, DMin, PhD, associate professor of Missions
and associate dean of Applied Ministry and Mentorship
Ida M. Bottoms Chair of Missions
Roy Fish School of Evangelism and Missions
Southwestern Baptist Theological Seminary

Church revitalization is a difficult work. It means restoring hope where hope is fleeing, leading toward a positive future where the present is bleak, and being patient when the need seems urgent. Few people understand all that revitalization entails, but Bill Henard does. In this work, he offers a workable strategy for revitalizing a church while also connecting with the insights and research of multiple other authors and practitioners. Keep this toolbox handy, as you will return to it over and over again.

Chuck Lawless, PhD, professor of Evangelism and Missions
dean of Doctrinal Studies
vice president for Spiritual Formation and Ministry Centers
Southeastern Baptist Theological Seminary
professor of Evangelism and Missions
dean of Doctrinal Studies
vice president for Spiritual Formation and Ministry Centers

ReClaimed Church presents a biblical, readable, and thorough roadmap for the critical work of church revitalization today.

Will Mancini, founder of Auxano
author of *God Dreams*

ReClaimed Church

BILL HENARD

ReClaimed Church

How Churches Grow, Decline,
and Experience Revitalization

PUBLISHING GROUP
NASHVILLE, TENNESSEE

978-1-4627-9071-5

Published by B&H Publishing Group
Nashville, Tennessee

Dewey Decimal Classification: 254.5
Subject Heading: CHURCH MEMBERSHIP \ CHURCH GROWTH
\ CHURCH RENEWAL

Cover photo © Cleve Persinger.

1 2 3 4 5 6 7 8 • 22 21 20 19 18

Always to my family
For whom I am
Indelibly grateful.
I am a man greatly blessed
To have a wife, children, and grandchildren
Who are my Joy.

One cannot imagine the incredible encouragement
That comes when a grandchild tells you that
They do not know what life would be like without you
Or when they scream with a shrill voice your name when they see you
Or when they find happiness in beating you in a video game
Or when they draw pictures for you of your favorite things.

I am extraordinarily proud of the adults my children have become
At how they love Christ
And how they serve Him in ministry and daily life.

Acknowledgments

I am grateful for many individuals and groups who have made this book project possible. First, I want to thank the West Virginia Convention of Southern Baptists for giving me the opportunity to research, study, and write in preparation for this book's release. The Convention has been extremely supportive as I have undertaken this project. Additionally, my Convention staff has been invaluable. I want to be careful in naming names, but Cleve Persinger was especially helpful, as he worked with me on developing both the graphic concepts and the graphics themselves. He, Tim Turner, and Danny Rumple are not only prodigious team members but friends and encouragers.

I am thankful to have worked with Taylor Combs on this project. Taylor served as my editor, but more than that, he grew up in my church in Lexington, Kentucky. His father was especially generous with me, taking me on numerous occasions to play golf. I even played with Taylor long before he would hit the ball three hundred yards. Now to see where God has brought him is amazing and a double blessing for me.

I am also indebted to Kenneth E. Priddy, executive director of the GO Center and president of The Ken Priddy Group. Some of the ideas for helping churches recognize where they are on the Life Stage originated with him. I have used this material in teaching churches about revitalization and found it extremely helpful, especially for those churches or individuals who were either in a state of denial or were unaware of their actual situation. I took his ideas and expanded, updated, and rewrote them, seeking to use my own study in developing them further. When I contacted him about permission to use his material, he wrote, "The bottom line for me is to see the evangelical church gain vitality in gathering the harvest, so if my material helps in your journey, feel free."[1] I am honored to use his material and to be allowed to add this critical information to this book.

The same graciousness can be said about Bill Day of the New Orleans Baptist Theological Seminary. I contacted Dr. Day about some research he had conducted, and he responded quickly and with kindness. These types of situations demonstrate the passion that church leaders have in helping the church. The issue is far more about Kingdom work than it is about personal profit. I find that attitude refreshing.

Finally, I am grateful for the opportunities I have had to teach church revitalization, not only on the seminary campus, but in churches and in the larger contexts of church associations and conventions. Much of this material was developed and honed as I engaged churches with their need to revitalize and replant, along with meeting others much wiser than I who understood the nuances of revitalization. Always the teacher . . . Always the student.

Contents

Foreword

From his pastor's study he stares out the window on Sunday morning looking at the parking lot. He knows every car in the lot. And he knows who drives every car in the lot. It wasn't many years ago that the same parking lot was overflowing. Members had to park on the street. And every week he would see new cars in that lot with new families walking toward the church building. But those days are long gone. Now the parking lot, like most of the church, is half empty on Sunday.

He takes one more look at the sermon notes and he places them back in his Bible and begins to walk that familiar path from his office to the pulpit. He remembers when these hallways were filled with young families and children but today—like every Sunday—he passes unused classrooms and a nearly empty nursery. As he stands and looks out across the congregation each week, he sees more and more empty pews and fewer and fewer faces. It's not because he doesn't love the Lord. It's not because he doesn't believe in the power of the Scriptures. It's not because he no longer preaches the good news of the gospel. Why is it so hard here when it wasn't as hard just a few years ago?

This is not an isolated story. This incident plays out tens of thousands of times across North America each and every Sunday morning. As many as seven out of ten churches across North America are in decline. Many of them in deep and rapid decline. Many of these churches are led by godly men who love the church, love their Savior, who believe the Bible, yet remain frustrated and discouraged that this church which they love and work so hard for continues to decline. In

my role as the director of church replanting for the North American
Mission Board of the Southern Baptist Convention I encounter these
churches all across North America. Churches that once thrived within
their communities and experienced growth now working hard just to
stop the bleeding. And a growing number of these churches each year
will close their doors. In my own denomination, we realize the loss of
more than nine hundred congregations each and every year. Many of
these churches have tried various programs and approaches to grow
their numbers and stop the decline. And many of these churches continue to decline. Churches today often find themselves in the midst
of communities that seem to transform overnight. Once a part of the
fabric of the community, many churches realize the faces in the pews
look nothing like those in the neighborhood. These churches struggle
to keep up with a rapidly changing demographic. And honestly, some
of them finally resign themselves to a slow decline and what may seem
to be an inevitable death.

It is into this environment of frustration and discouragement
that Dr. Bill Henard brings real hope and optimism to the task of
reclaiming the church. Drawing on his own personal experiences and
years of study and profound knowledge of this subject, Dr. Henard
has provided a timely and targeted resource for the church in North
America today. Born out of a solid theological foundation and proven
practical application, this book provides a pathway of real and lasting
hope for churches. This book is not simply warmed over and worn
out programmatic approaches to church growth. This book provides
a solid biblical approach to guiding a church to the future that Jesus
offers to any church that seeks His plan and glory. This book is born
out of the crucible of working in the trenches to battle for the local
church. Dr. Henard understands the struggle and the frustration faced
by declining churches, and more importantly, he knows how to lead
that church through that crucible to a future that is designed not by the
program of men but by Jesus the chief Shepherd of that local church.

With a heart for pastors and a deep love and respect for the importance and ministry of the local church, *ReClaimed Church* is certain to
become a cherished resource in your library. I commend this work to
every pastor, every leader, and every church member who longs for the

day once again when their church is a center of evangelistic activity and disciple-making excellence.

Mark Clifton
senior director of Church Replanting
North American Mission Board SBC

Introduction

ReClaimed — rə'klāmd verb: retrieve or recover (something previously lost, given, or paid); obtain the return of. Synonyms: get back, recoup, claim back, recover, regain, retrieve. Recover (material) for reuse; recycle.[1]

My daughter Virginia loves to spend time ReClaiming old furniture. She has familiarized herself with quality furniture names and is fairly astute in recognizing valuable pieces. She has ReClaimed some dressers and china cabinets that have turned out quite nicely. One antique she found was in the old country store building that my father-in-law owned and operated decades ago. This Hoosier cabinet is a valuable piece of furniture as an antique, and it carries a great deal of sentimental value. The cabinet, though, is a wreck. Several coats of paint cover the wood where someone obviously tried to fix the scratches and imperfections. One door is off and may not be salvageable. When I saw it, I wanted to put it out of its misery. My daughter, conversely, envisions what it could be, not just what it is.

I have a feeling that the image of the Hoosier cabinet is the image that many people have about the church. It is time to put it out of its misery. Members have tried to paint over its scratches and imperfections, but now the paint is peeling and has lost its luster. Its spiritual doors are off their hinges, and no one knows if they are even salvageable. Nobody has much hope for the established church. It cannot be ReClaimed. I, however, take an opposite position.

Have you ever seen anyone use ReClaimed wood? My father-in-law's store provided dozens of boards that could be resanded, refinished, and reused in a house or office and provide not just a nostalgic look, but some high-quality wall and floor boards not usually found today. All they needed was to be ReClaimed. I believe the established church is ReClaimable just like a valuable piece of wood.

Here is the proof. As I have studied and read about church revitalization, one of the reoccurring themes is the Life Stage.[2] The typical graphic for the Life Stage is a bell curve that tracks a church's birth, plateau, and decline. I discovered this bell curve years ago when I read Robert Dale's book *To Dream Again*.[3] In my opinion, his ideas were ahead of his time and mostly overlooked or misunderstood. Today, numerous authors and seminar leaders use this model in some form or fashion.

A church's Life Stage, though, is far more complex than birth, plateau, and death. In fact, unless intentionally planted, most churches do not experience birth in the same way. Even intentional church plants may have different reasons for a church being started in a particular place. Each of these scenarios plays into the Life Stage of the church.

Additionally, how the church grows determines its place on the Life Stage. A church can have a correct starting point but head into struggle because its next steps are skewed, faulty, or even downright sinful. These specifics must come into focus when evaluating and considering church revitalization.

I first encountered the need for church revitalization when I moved to Alabama to pastor a large but declining church in a transitioning community. "White flight" was becoming the norm. Deep-seated racism was rooted in the hearts of many people on both sides of the issue. One of the things that alarmed me the most was watching some of the largest churches of the 1950s close their doors in the 1990s. It seemed the only ones that could survive were those that relocated, and even some of them waited too late. I could see that scenario playing out in the church that I now served. To be honest, the only reason that I went there was because I sensed a deep call from God to go and help that church. It was, for me at least, a Macedonian call. The church was an intentional church plant in 1955. The reason, however, is suspect. Presumably, another church in the same general area did not want people of a different economic status to attend their church. Therefore, they started this church for these people from "the other side of the tracks."

That perspective and history permeated the church. Some of the resistance, hesitancy, and distrust could be understood when viewed through the lens of the past. Everybody seemed to know it, but nobody wanted to talk about it. The condition of the church, candidly, was above my pay grade. I had not been trained how to pastor a church that should have been climbing the growth side of the bell curve but instead was struggling both on the outside and on the inside. In fact, the pastor search committee took me to the next suburb over to show me houses. I knew there were issues because none of those people were going to drive to our church. I do not think the committee was being dishonest; I think it was symptomatic of the denial that many members were experiencing. The neighborhood was changing, and no one knew what to do about it.

Thus, the need for a paradigm shift away from the traditional growth bell curve and toward a graphic that would better chart the various ways that churches grow, plateau, and decline was realized. One reason churches struggle in revitalization is that they approach the task through a "cookie-cutter" process; but churches, like people, are not all the same.

The intention of *ReClaimed Church* with a new Life Stage process is to equip churches to discover their individual nuances, characteristics, and history that not only make them unique, but also give insight into why they are at this precise stage in their existence.

Churches, regardless of their history, mistakes, or poor decisions, can redirect themselves into growth. The task is not an easy one, but church leaders must be committed to revitalizing churches and getting them healthy. It is important, if the evangelical church is going to reach the world with the gospel, that a church planting revolution takes place. For that transformation to happen, churches must be healthy. Healthy churches plant healthy churches. Unhealthy churches do not plant unhealthy churches. They usually just die.

> Unhealthy churches do not plant unhealthy churches. They usually just die.

The solution is to focus on church ReClaimed. How do we take a church that is unhealthy and at the end of its Life Stage and get it on mission again? The answer is to for the church to be ReClaimed. The church—just like an old piece of furniture—can be ReClaimed and have more value now than ever before.

ReClaimed Church offers a process by which a congregation can reassess, rethink, realign, revise, and reaffirm its identity, strategy, vision, and goals in order to become a viable, growing church once again. This idea is not a magic formula; it is a process that can help a declining church rediscover its purpose and mission. The foundation for any church to be ReClaimed is the Word of God and the preaching of the Word. Do not miss that fact. With preaching, though, comes careful application. Haddon Robinson wrote, "More heresy is preached in application than in Bible exegesis."[4] With that understanding, it is absolutely true that application is essential to the art of preaching. R. Albert Mohler explained this thought when he argued,

> Application of biblical truth is a necessary task of expository preaching. But application must follow the diligent and disciplined task of explaining the text itself. T. H. L. Parker describes preaching like this: "Expository preaching consists in the explanation and application of a passage of Scripture. Without explanation it is not expository; without application it is not preaching."[5]

Take careful note of the balance of these two perspectives. Revitalization is grounded in the Word of God; its application is rooted in the principles that are drawn from Scripture. This book is about the application of biblical truth to the church so that the church may become the ReClaimed Church.

The Life Stages
of the Church

CHAPTER 1

The Birth Stage:
Vision or Crisis?

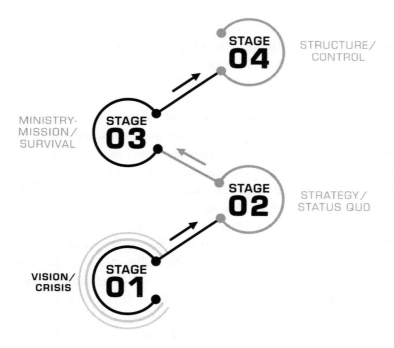

Perhaps the most important, yet most ignored, part of a church's existence is its birth stage. Every diagram I have observed of the Life Stage of the church focuses only on one specific way in which a church is birthed. It starts out of the vision, dreams, or goals of a group of people who desire to reach a certain demographic of the population.

While many churches begin in this fashion, scores of churches have been founded through much more ominous beginnings. Many churches began because of a split, a splinter, or a bias. Additionally, while a church may have a strong starting point, long before it reaches the plateau after a strong growth and development phase, it can begin to make poor choices in leadership, structure, and strategy. These poor choices set the direction for the church, early in its existence, toward failure. In order for a church to be ReClaimed, it must understand its Life Stage, and specifically how it was founded.

Most church plants hopefully began out of a vision that a pastor, a church, or a group of individuals had to start a new congregation in another part of their city or in another town that was unchurched. That scenario is not always true. Let me share the beginnings of the previous two churches I served as senior pastor.

One church was located in a large city in the Deep South. The story of its origin was shared with me by members who had been a part of the church from the time of its launch. They were attending a fairly prominent church in town but traveled from the "other side of the tracks" to get there. The church leaders were not particularly enthused to have folks of a lower socioeconomic status attending, becoming members, and moving into leadership. Therefore, they decided to plant a church for those who fell within this economic criterion in the neighborhood where most of them lived. The church grew and thrived for a time, but there was always this nagging stigma of being a "poor, blue-collar" church. That mind-set affected outreach, decision-making, and vision. Oftentimes, they were short-sighted, I believe, because of their tainted beginnings. Their history served as a reminder that, in the opinion of some, they did not measure up. Today, although the church has relocated, they are developing plans to dissolve and merge with another congregation. Their problems are obviously not just rooted in the past; how they were birthed certainly set the stage for possible decline.

The other church was birthed intentionally by a local pastor and a group of laypeople. More than a hundred years ago, a group of people began a prayer meeting on their side of town. No evangelical church existed where they lived. They found another group of people nearby who were also praying together regularly. Eventually, they approached their pastor about helping them start a church with these two groups. The pastor agreed and his church provided the assistance and the people necessary to have a successful church launch. The richness of their history offers a heritage upon which they can continue to build. It began with a vision, and that vision allows the church to re-vision itself as change becomes necessary.

First Steps

The first step to a ReClaimed Church is to examine the history of the church and to ask how those beginnings affect the attitude, behavior, and response of the church leadership, in particular, and the church at large in general. Attitude is one of the keys to church revitalization. If the church has a bad attitude or a defeatist attitude, it may never see the potential it actually has.

The Fix

The question everyone is going to ask is: How do I fix this problem? Listen to the words of the apostle Paul in Philippians 3:12–16:

Not that I have already reached the goal or am already perfect, but I make every effort to take hold of it because I also have been taken hold of by Christ Jesus. Brothers and sisters, I do not consider myself to have taken hold of it. But one thing I do: Forgetting what is behind and reaching forward to what is ahead, I pursue as my goal the prize promised by God's heavenly call in Christ Jesus. Therefore, let all of us who are mature think this way. And if you think differently about anything, God will reveal this also to you. In any case, we should live up to whatever truth we have attained.

The answer is simple and yet complex. The church must accept its past and embrace the past's importance, but it must also move beyond its limitations. Churches and pastors make the mistake of either criticizing the past or trying to ignore it altogether. The past is the past. How the church started is how the church started. Therefore, the church's beginnings should be used as an advantage. Look at what Paul says: *Forgetting what is behind and reaching forward to what is ahead.* What is Paul suggesting? Here are some thoughts:

1. Do not transfer the past to the future. In whatever way that the church began, good or bad, do not live in the past and do not allow the past to determine the future. Learn from the past, interact with the past, honor the past and those who are/were a part of it, but do not dwell in the past. If necessary, lead the church through a time to honor the past, but make a clear decision to move forward. When the past is mentioned, honor it but do not allow it to be pertinent in decision-making or vision-casting. Lead the church through a time in which they ask God to help them break the hold that the past has on them and then start moving forward. If the past includes some shameful behaviors or attitudes, seek God's healing for those times and find healing for the shame. God's forgiveness and love for the church is clear in Scripture. Remind the church that God has not forgotten them.

2. Allow the church to embrace its past but not hold onto it. If the church tries to ignore its beginnings, the church is only denying reality. Paul wrote, *Not that I have already reached the goal or am already perfect.* Instead of being embarrassed by how the church started or why the church started in the way that it did, embrace it. Lead the church to learn from its past and to be thankful for its founding and founders, but do not stay there. Those of us who are pro-life believe that even a child conceived in rape is still valuable in the eyes of God. While that child's conception is by no means a desired nor encouraged beginning, what a testimony that child and mother will have to a world that extols death and disregards life. Likewise, a church with the most problematic of beginnings is loved by God and is valuable in God's eyes.

3. Pursue God's future for the church with every ounce of energy. Paul declared, *I pursue as my goal the prize promised by God's heavenly call in Christ Jesus.* The church must reach the point of being dissatisfied with where it is presently. It cannot go back to the past or allow the past to keep the church defeated. God has a much grander plan than ominous beginnings. Richard Melick offers this explanation:

> Since the Greek athletic games captured the imagination of all of the peninsula, Macedonia included, it spoke vividly to the readers. The manner of attainment is explained by two

participles. First, "forgetting what is behind" comprehensively expresses Paul's future orientation. What was done was done! Both the nostalgia of the former life and the "good ole days" of his Christian life would paralyze him in terms of what God wanted in the future. Every day was a new adventure. Second, he was "straining toward what is ahead." This word continues the athletic metaphor. It is particularly graphic, bringing to mind the straining muscles, clear focus, and complete dedication of the runner in his race to the prize. Both mental and physical discipline were necessary.[1]

While Paul obviously is dealing with living a victorious Christian life, his words certainly apply to the victorious church. Know the past and understand the past, but find God's future for the church and pursue it with deep discipline and absolute commitment.

It is critical to understand a church's history and to lead the church to deal with its past, because the past may be why the church is struggling, fighting, and in decline. A church that was birthed out of a split oftentimes carries that same anger into the new start. Its only vision is to get away from the old church. Issues of bitterness, power struggles, and a lack of respect for the pastor and staff permeate the congregation. Sometimes the new pastor tries to lead the church into vision-casting and strategy, only to find that the leaders of the church thwart every effort. The reason is because they have not properly dealt with their past anger and perhaps personal sin and fault in the split. They may have an identity crisis because they know that their church was started out of bias, prejudice, or a sense of being unwanted. I do not want to over-analyze the issue, but in the same way the people personally struggle with identity, self-esteem, personal worth, and acceptance, so does the church. Know a church's past, and it will be advantageous in understanding its present and in planning for its future.

CHAPTER 2

Infant Stage: Strategy or Status Quo?

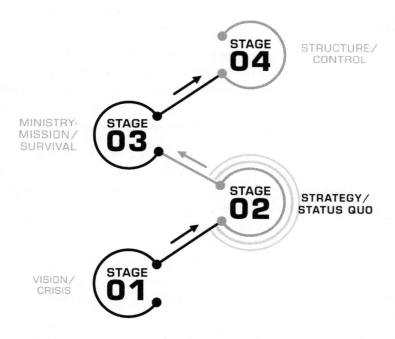

When a church begins in the right way, with a clear vision as to its purpose and future, it can then begin to develop its strategy. Strategy is crucial. It is the *how* to the *who* of our vision. The vision is who we are and aspire to be. It is the picture of the desired future. George Bullard identifies vision as the "current understanding of God's spiritual

strategic direction . . . cast by leadership and owned by membership."[1]
While many churches will develop both a vision statement (the dreaming stage) and a mission statement (the doing stage), the strategy phase
takes the mission and puts it into specific details. Vision asks: What will
the future look like as we fulfill our mission? Mission answers the question: What do we do succinctly? Strategy, then, is the chosen method
or plan for bringing about the stated vision through the mission. The
mission statement is a short, one-sentence synopsis of what the church
does. The vision statement is a lengthy outline of a clear, yet challenging
picture of the church's future. Aubrey Malphurs makes these two of many
distinctions:

1. The mission is used for planning where the church is going; the
   vision is used for communicating where the church is going.
2. A mission statement must be short enough to fit on a T-shirt.
   The vision statement, however, goes into detail and can range
   from a single paragraph to several pages in length.[2]

Thus, a church births and develops out of a clear vision that unfolds
through its mission statement. Momentum is built as people adopt the
vision as theirs and begin to live out the mission. Most church plants
become successful because they can implant a vision DNA into the life
of their members. The membership reflects the vision and fulfills the
mission.

As the church moves into infancy, a more specific strategy must be in
place in order for the vision and mission to come to fruition. The vision
tells us who we are and are going to be, the mission clarifies the action
of our vision, and now the strategy offers the specifics of how the church
will accomplish these things. For churches that started with a vision, this
next step is a natural part of their maturation. If only church work was
that easy . . .

If the church can move naturally to the strategy phase, it most probably will continue on a growth phase. Enter in, however, the status quo.
The status quo can hit any church at any time. It is the point of satisfaction for where the church is at its present state. While it may still embrace
its vision, it loses focus on a strategy that will be most effective in getting
the church to fulfill its mission and reach its vision.

A church in Birmingham launched an additional campus as a part of its vision to impact the city with the gospel. Initially, the second campus met in a school, requiring members to load and unload equipment weekly. Sunday started early and ended into the afternoon for volunteers. At first, those involved were excited. Showing up at 7:00 a.m. was new and invigorating. After about a year, that excitement turned into drudgery. While the congregation saw growth and baptisms, the core group desired a more permanent location. The vision became cloudy, and the willingness to compromise set in. A building was secured, and once the congregation got settled, the worship center was full. At the school, it was quite evident that growth was possible and necessary, but at the new building, the 80 percent rule was in effect.[3] The vision to impact the city was still believed but not quite impassioned. Instead of developing new strategies for moving forward with their mission, the status quo set in. They became satisfied. The building became the mission, and the original mission all but died.

Status quo sets in for several reasons:

1. Church growth is difficult. Evangelism in the twenty-first century is more challenging than it has ever been in most parts of the world. Back in 2003, Thom Rainer wrote a book entitled *The Unchurched Next Door*. I have quoted from that book extensively in sermons and on seminary campuses. He says that, overall, the unchurched are not anti-church and are not strongly antagonistic to the gospel, citing that 5 percent of American adults are highly resistant to the gospel and another 21 percent are somewhat resistant.[4] Jump ahead less than fifteen years, and those numbers have most probably increased, at least in the highly resistant group. Anecdotally, one need only to watch a few news broadcasts or peruse the Internet to discover that, worldwide, there is an increased disdain for Christianity. Certainly, much of the visibility is due to the easy access that most people have with the Internet and social media. It also appears that the world has become much angrier and is willing to vocalize that anger. In most cities, initiative/cold-call evangelism is far less effective and even a negative in many cases. Most churches do not have week-long evangelistic meetings or revivals anymore. Evangelism has moved more personal and relational, and many Christians are not spiritually prepared to initiate gospel conversations. For established churches, they are ingrained in a particular methodology, and learning and implementing a new methodology is extremely difficult. Thus, the status quo sets in. It is easier to stay as we are than to risk rejection, even if our vision says that we are risk takers.

2. Church growth creates the appearance of an impersonal church. Once a church starts growing, it can reach a certain size so that members do not know everyone who is attending. Growth may require multiple services or overflow areas. It may demand moving away from a single Bible study hour to multiple Bible study groups that meet at various times during the week. Many people lack adaptability, and these growth-induced changes can make them feel uncomfortable. Even new churches can reach a level of comfort that causes them to resist additional growth. Unfortunately, the motive for some church planting is not to reach an unreached segment of the population, but to keep the sponsor church from growing any more.

3. Church growth is messy. One church with which I was consulting had fallen into the status quo. In one of the first meetings I had with their leadership and other church members, I was touring the church facilities on a Wednesday evening. As we walked into the worship area, a lady carried with her a thirty-two-ounce soda cup. One of the primary leaders turned to her and scolded her for such a heinous act. I immediately thought to myself, *No wonder they are declining*. The status quo was more about personal preference than reaching people. If new people came and had children who did not know how to behave or if a non-Christian had too many questions or a single girl arrived with tattoos and purple hair, it would create a mess! Status quo is much easier than messiness, especially if the church has reached its initial goals.

Sam Rainer gives an excellent synopsis of why churches fall into the status quo and the resulting consequences of that action. He writes:

Here's why the status quo is so tempting . . . and dangerous.

The status quo opposes more. Every church should seek to reach more people and go to more places. The temptation of the status quo is that you can be satisfied with the current mission footprint of a church. The danger is that people do not hear the gospel because you were supposed to go and reach them. Most people that push for the status quo are wanting to stay put, and I'm not aware of the biblical mandate "just stay put."

The status quo is highly contagious. Have you ever been part of a meeting in which a lot of effort was exerted for nothing? Then someone speaks up and says, "Let's wrap this up and reconvene later." And everyone quickly agrees. It's easy to convince people to stay the same. It's harder to get them to change. And that's why too many church meetings end with few, if any, action items.

The status quo discourages risk. One of the great temptations of leadership is to build a culture of maintaining the status quo. When people don't expect big things, then even little things seem like grand accomplishments. Church leaders can feel quite good about themselves when everyone congratulates the little accomplishments. It's easy to neglect big things when you're receiving a steady stream of praise for the little things. The danger is status quo churches will miss the grand rewards of great risks for the kingdom.

The status quo encourages complacency. If everyone is happy with the way things are, then why go and upset people? The danger is God doesn't call people to happiness. The status quo is completely inward. It focuses on people already in the body without considering those who need to be reached.

The status quo leaves people unprepared for disruption. The struggle between good and evil will play out in your congregation—somehow, some way, and at some point. It's inevitable—there will be a disruption, even if you work hard to prevent it. Status quo leaders leave their people unprepared for what will inevitably occur. You might as well go ahead and build a culture that expects disruptions because they happen.[5]

Falling into the status quo is an immense threat for every church. When a congregation reaches its initial goals, hits the proverbial growth wall, or gets to a particular age or level of comfort, leaders will be tempted to take a greater possession of the church, especially if they are the ones who helped birth it. Even churches that had an intentional launch can quickly find themselves on a plateau because of the temptation of the status quo.

CHAPTER 3

The Adolescent Stage: Ministry or Survival?

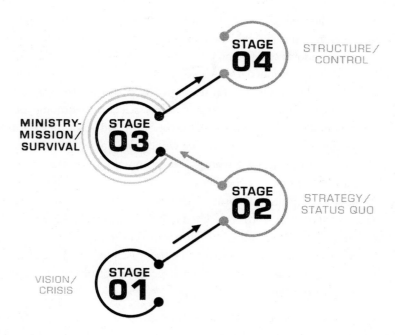

As the church continues to move into growth, it must develop ministry and mission that strengthen the church internally and align the church externally. A key component to church revitalization and initiating change is getting the church onto the mission field to minister through the gospel and meeting needs.[1] Leadership must learn to strike the balance between developing ministry that cares for the church and getting the church onto the mission field.

When ministry and mission begin, leadership learns to give things away. The pastors do not do all the visiting or care. People are encouraged and trained to become decision-makers and are allowed the freedom to try and to fail. The church moves beyond its four walls to engage the culture with greater relevance and impact. The congregation becomes more gospel-centered in its approach to growth, health, and ministry.

Acts 6:1–7 provides the classic example:

> In those days, as the disciples were increasing in number, there arose a complaint by the Hellenistic Jews against the Hebraic Jews that their widows were being overlooked in the daily distribution. The Twelve summoned the whole company of the disciples and said, "It would not be right for us to give up preaching the word of God to wait on tables. Brothers and sisters, select from among you seven men of good reputation, full of the Spirit and wisdom, whom we can appoint to this duty. But we will devote ourselves to prayer and to the ministry of the word." This proposal pleased the whole company. So they chose Stephen, a man full of faith and the Holy Spirit, and Philip, Prochorus, Nicanor, Timon, Parmenas, and Nicolaus, a convert from Antioch. They had them stand before the apostles, who prayed and laid their hands on them.
>
> So the word of God spread, the disciples in Jerusalem increased greatly in number, and a large group of priests became obedient to the faith.

While there are many scholars, including myself, who view this passage as a precursor to the deacons mentioned in 1 Timothy 3, the primary emphasis of the passage is how the early church faced the challenge of meeting needs or possibly plateauing. I believe that idea is the point made by the apostles. They essentially served as the pastors of the Jerusalem church, although that ministry role had also not yet been fully developed. The need was more than financial. The church was experiencing a cultural divide between the Hebraic and Hellenistic widows. The Hebrew-speaking widows' needs were being met while the Greek speakers were being neglected. It was a moment of ministry crisis. The disciples' declaration in Acts 6:2, "It would not be right for us to give up preaching the word of God to wait on tables," is a clear declaration of the means of growth in the early church. If they stopped the ministry of the Word, the church would stop growing. Therefore, they developed a ministry plan that would meet the widows' needs and also allow the church to remain on a growth plain.

Luke lets us know that the plan was not only successful but far-reaching, for he declares, "So the word of God spread, the disciples in Jerusalem increased greatly in number, and a large group of priests became obedient to the faith" (6:7). It would have been an incredible story at this point if the priests were some of the Sadducean priests, but they were most probably a part of the eight thousand-plus common priests who received little or no support from the temple. Luke's mention of this occurrence must have been a significant issue because the "next event would be Stephen's arrest and his stirring critique of the temple. Some of these priestly 'insiders' may have shared the same viewpoint and longed for a purer worship of God."[2] In other words, when the Word is preached and genuine ministry needs are met, even some of the most difficult people come to Christ. In a world where evangelism is becoming more difficult, every pastor must remember that principle.

Acts 7–8 also offers insight into the importance of mission. After the martyrdom of Stephen, persecution arose in Jerusalem, so that "all except the apostles were scattered throughout the land of Judea and Samaria. Devout men buried Stephen and mourned deeply over him. Saul, however, was ravaging the church. He would enter house after house, drag off men and women, and put them in prison" (8:1–3). It would be through this diaspora that the church would begin to fulfill the Great Commission. Up until this point, the church had remained in Jerusalem, experiencing incredible success, as "the number of the disciples multiplied greatly" (Acts 6:7 ESV). At the offset, three thousand people were saved and baptized. After the teaching of Simon Peter and John, Luke mentions that five thousand men believed (Acts 4:4). How many of the original three thousand and now the five thousand returned home following these conversions is unknown, but little doubt exists that the Jerusalem church had grown quite large. It could easily have moved into the status quo, as evidenced by the widows' crisis of Acts 6. The church was large enough, some might have said. The church must take care of its own (a true statement but one that comes with the qualification and interpretation of self-preservation).

So now enters the ministry of Acts 6 and God's allowance of persecution in Acts 8. The church either learns to give the ministry away and to get onto the mission field, or the church moves toward plateau. MacArthur offers this observation:

> Therefore, in spite of the persecution, those believers who had been scattered were not cowering somewhere in fear but went about preaching the word. They had been doing so before the outbreak of the persecution, and after being scattered they continued to preach. "Went about" is from *dierchomai,* a word used frequently in Acts of missionary endeavors (8:40; 9:32; 13:6; 14:24; 15:3, 41; 16:6; 18:23; 19:1, 21; 20:2).
>
> "Preaching" is from *euangelizō,* which refers to proclaiming the gospel. All the scattered believers were involved in evangelism. Although some are specially gifted as evangelists (Acts 21:8; Eph. 4:11; 2 Tim. 4:5), all Christians are called to proclaim Christ.[3]

The Word continues to spread, and even Saul the persecutor surrenders to Christ. By Acts 11, the mission had reached Antioch. Luke records:

> Now those who had been scattered as a result of the persecution that started because of Stephen made their way as far as Phoenicia, Cyprus, and Antioch, speaking the word to no one except Jews. But there were some of them, men from Cyprus and Cyrene, who came to Antioch and began speaking to the Greeks also, proclaiming the good news about the Lord Jesus. The Lord's hand was with them, and a large number who believed turned to the Lord. News about them reached the church in Jerusalem, and they sent out Barnabas to travel as far as Antioch. When he arrived and saw the grace of God, he was glad and encouraged all of them to remain true to the Lord with devoted hearts, for he was a good man, full of the Holy Spirit and of faith. And large numbers of people were added to the Lord.

Then he went to Tarsus to search for Saul, and when he found him he brought him to Antioch. For a whole year they met with the church and taught large numbers. The disciples were first called Christians at Antioch. (Acts 11:19–26)

It would be the Antioch church that would then send Paul and Barnabas on the first commissioned missionary journey. Notice that the church at Antioch grew just as the church at Jerusalem had grown in this early stage of its existence. Luke again records:

When the Gentiles heard this, they rejoiced and honored the word of the Lord, and all who had been appointed to eternal life believed. The word of the Lord spread through the whole region. But the Jews incited the prominent God-fearing women and the leading men of the city. They stirred up persecution against Paul and Barnabas and expelled them from their district. But Paul and Barnabas shook the dust off their feet against them and went to Iconium. And the disciples were filled with joy and the Holy Spirit. (Acts 13:48–52)

Growth, mission, and ministry go together, even when coupled with severe persecution. The church that wants to avoid the crises, problems, and difficulties of ministry and mission moves into a survival mode. Ministry becomes more about taking care of those in the status quo than meeting genuine needs. Mission is nonexistent unless it provides an opportunity for self-promotion or self-worth. In other words, the church in the state of self-preservation will feel good about itself if it helps others in need, but the motive is far more self than it is mission or ministry.

For example, I was talking with the staff member of a church that had been on a decade-long plateau. No one really noticed the plateau because the church had regular baptisms and additions. They just did not notice that they were only maintaining, not growing. Most of the leadership was satisfied because they were growing old together with their church friends. The numbers, though, did not lie.

Leadership would even talk about mission. They were proud that a group had gone to another country one time a decade ago. Locally, they fed the hungry. In fact, they would load up the buses and pick up the homeless downtown for a Thanksgiving meal, then herd all the partakers into the sanctuary to hear a sermon from the pastor, and then load them back up on the buses to be driven "home" to their downtown box on the street. This staff member relayed to me that the church bragged on this work as though it was something noble. He also quickly mentioned that they ceased the ministry when they caught a couple of homeless men wandering around the church during the dinner and thought it to be too risky from that point on. It was mission, but it was mission with an asterisk, a qualification that its purpose was far more for the church than for the mission.

At this point, even if it does not recognize this stage, the church has moved into a survival mode. Decisions certainly become more about what is best for the church at hand than about reaching those outside of Christ. Risk becomes an anomaly. The church, though it has grown in the past, now decides it is time to survive. Even if the church develops a strategy of how it would continue to grow, that strategy is ignored when the church realizes that it must give the ministry away and move out of its newfound comfort zone. As long as those who do the ministry can keep doing the ministry, everyone is happy. The church of seventy-five can expect that the pastor makes all of the visits. Let that church grow to 175 or 275, and the scenario dramatically changes. Now the youth pastor appears at the hospital before surgery, the Bible study teacher calls absentees, and the deacons are expected to care for the widows, and nobody likes it. Therefore, the church locks down, and instead of expanding ministry and mission, it reverts to its past when the "apostles" took care of everybody and did the preaching as well.

The saying "small church mentality" may be overused and sometimes misused, but at this juncture on the growth plane, it is incredibly important. Why is it that most churches have fewer than a hundred attendees? In fact, the median church in America has seventy-five attendees[4] and 59 percent of churches have less than one hundred attendees on a given Sunday.[5] Some of the reasons include location and population, but even in the more rural or small-town areas, a church probably has more potential than it is reaching. The church is not growing because it does not want to grow any larger and has moved into a survival mode. It is now purposed to take care of itself. This fact is true for long, established churches, but it is also true for many newer church plants. Any church can start out right and have the right goals, vision, and even strategy. The real test occurs when the church has to expand its leadership base and ministry concepts. It either decides to develop ministry to meet needs and mission to reach the world, or it chooses to hunker down and take care of itself. When a church decides to become a survivor, it unfortunately sets the stage for death.

CHAPTER 4

The Adult Stage: Structure or Conflict/Control?

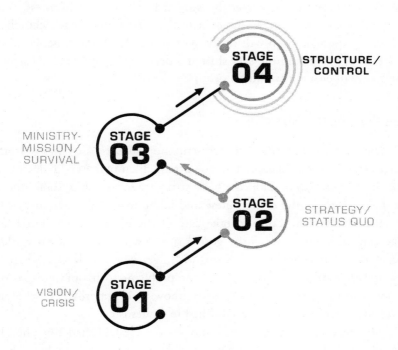

STAGE **04**   STRUCTURE/ CONTROL

MINISTRY- MISSION/ SURVIVAL   STAGE **03**

STAGE **02**   STRATEGY/ STATUS QUO

VISION/ CRISIS   STAGE **01**

T he church is always developing structure. In the early stages, that structure is quite fluid and basic. As the church grows and matures, it reaches that point when it must decide to structure itself for continued growth. If there is no structure, the church reaches the point that it cannot maintain the attendance. Therefore, it begins to decline.

Structure is far more than just the development of having a pastor, worship service, and Bible study groups. Structure, at this point, provides a foundation for the church to grow larger numerically and spiritually. It is rooted in how the church will provide ministry, how it will be on mission, and how it will administrate the functions of the church. While every church desires to be deeply spiritual, it must learn to handle more than just spiritual issues. As budgets increase, as the church grows older, and as members have a greater investment in the church business, this stage on the growth plane becomes critical. It is here that many churches that have experienced growth in the past will slide into decline, because they cannot make the necessary shift and decisions to implement a structure that will ensure the church's future growth.

Healthy Church Structure

The necessity of healthy church structure has been a challenge from the time the church began. It is not a new dilemma. Acts 2 describes how the first church developed a basic structure for worship, Bible study, and fellowship. As the church grew and additional challenges surfaced, the leaders added structure to take care of the need. As the church at large continued to grow, as the gospel spread across the known world, and as the church began to mature with age, new problems appeared. The apostle Paul addressed some of the problems to his protégé pastor Timothy in his personal letter that we know as 1 Timothy. The church being addressed was the one established in Ephesus.

Paul, accompanied by Aquila and Priscilla, established this church around AD 52 (Acts 18:18–26). He did not remain there long, but returned in AD 54 to serve as pastor of the congregation until AD 57 (Acts 19). After his first Roman imprisonment, he would leave Timothy in Ephesus in AD 63 to address problems and issues that had arisen during the time of the church's existence. Paul would write his first epistle to Timothy most probably from Macedonia.[1]

At this juncture, the church was no longer a church plant. It was an established church of eleven years and was facing the problems that churches face when proper structure is not in place or when faulty structure exists. According to 1 Timothy, the church Timothy inherited faced difficulties with doctrine (1:3–7), worship (2:1–15), leadership (3:1–13), and money (6:6–19). If a proper structure was not put into place and followed, those problems would fester and eventually lead the church into decline. Unfortunately for Ephesus, Timothy would not remain very long with the congregation. By the time the church at Ephesus is mentioned again in Scripture some forty years after its birth, it became known as the church that had left their first love (Rev. 2:1–7). It may seem like a giant hermeneutical leap to go from the need for structure to a loss of love for Christ, each other, and the lost, but this one fact demonstrates why so many churches are in trouble. Instead of structuring for growth, they become cesspools of power struggles and fights over position. The issues root themselves far more in a spiritual structure than just in a physical structure. In other words, a church can have the right schematic that has a proven growth record, but if the foundational spiritual structure is not in place, the structure will lead to control, not growth.

Therefore, look to the Scripture. Paul gives a clear picture of healthy structure in 1 Timothy. In fact, he provides crucial insight into how to get a church back on target to grow again (although I do not want us to get ahead of ourselves). What does a healthy, spiritual, and foundational structure look like?

1. The church must be grounded in the Word so that its decision-making, doctrine, and practice are biblically based (1:1–11). Most churches will claim to be biblically based. They will have in their constitution and by-laws a Statement of Faith or a Confessional Statement. They will expect biblical sermons and will use the Bible in their Sunday school or small groups ministry. The problem is that the Bible not only does not play into the daily lives of the church, but it has not been applied to certain areas of the church. For example, for churches that maintain a congregational-approval governance, how many horror stories have been told about churches getting into fights during business meetings? We only want to believe the Bible until it condemns our carnality.

Mark Dever, in his book *What Is a Healthy Church?*, defines a healthy church as "a congregation that increasingly reflects God's character as his character has been revealed in his Word."[2] Being healthy is much more than just a performance of duties on the outside. It is a reflection of what we have become on the inside as a result of God's transforming grace and power.

2. The church must develop healthy leaders (3:1–7). The Bible gives some clear guidance as to the proper governance of the church, but Paul's admonition to pastors/elders and deacons is far more than just the establishment of particular offices. It is why he warns, "Don't be too quick to appoint anyone as an elder" (5:22). I am afraid that I have been guilty of this mistake. In my enthusiasm to see men step into leadership, both as paid and as volunteer leaders, I did not examine them well enough, and not just through an ordination council. I am afraid that the red flags of their behavior were present, but I did not hold them up to a particular standard first. The fact is, if someone is not a faithful church member, that person will not be a faithful pastor or leader. If a man is not fully committed while serving as a layman, he probably will not be faithful once he moves into leadership. In other words, if he does not like attending and serving faithfully as a volunteer, he won't like attending and serving faithfully in an official capacity. The point of this study is that the church must be structured so that it has accountability measures in place in order to produce, hire, and maintain healthy leaders.

Paul, in 1 Timothy 3, makes it clear that the evidence of this health can be seen in and proven through several areas:

- Healthy leaders lead their families well.
- Healthy leaders lead moral lifestyles.
- Healthy leaders lead through a godly testimony.
- Healthy leaders love to serve.
- Healthy leaders love to be spiritually challenged.
- Healthy leaders love to share their faith.
- Healthy leaders allow what they believe to affect what they do.

A church cannot and will not have a healthy structure if it is not developing healthy leaders.

3. The church must be structured to help believers grow to a maturity that challenges them to lead. They may never be called upon to fulfill an official church position, but they need to lead nonetheless. That is the point of 1 Timothy 4. The reasons are numerous:

I. Healthy Christians know how to discern true and false doctrine. It is interesting that the longer we are exposed to certain ideas, thoughts, or beliefs, the more those ideas become ours, even when in the beginning we said no to them. One of the primary ways that Satan defeats us is through subtlety. If he reveals his plans too quickly, we will easily see that his plans are not of God, but if we are slowly exposed to them, we may eventually accept these ideas as being true.

A healthy church structure facilitates believers to know and apply Scripture so that they avoid false doctrine and false behavior. An unhealthy church structure allows only for certain leaders to know these things, thus leading to a super-spiritualism among some. The church's leaders can't be hoarders; biblical doctrine is necessary for all Christians.

II. Healthy Christians become disciples who make disciples. What are the characteristics of a disciple who makes disciples? Paul points out some of the qualifications, especially as he addresses Timothy personally in 4:11–16:

> Command and teach these things. Don't let anyone despise your youth, but set an example for the believers in speech, in conduct, in love, in faith, and in purity. Until I come, give your attention to public reading, exhortation, and teaching. Don't neglect the gift that is in you; it was given to you through prophecy, with the laying on of hands by the council of elders. Practice these things; be committed to them, so that your progress may be evident to all. Pay close attention to your life and your teaching; persevere in these things, for in doing this you will save both yourself and your hearers.

Just like Paul encouraged Timothy to practice the use of his gifts both for his own sake and the sake of his hearers, we ought to use our spiritual gifts in order to be disciples, and to make disciples.

III. Healthy Christians are committed to personal godliness and worship. Instead of consuming gossip or spiritual junk food, Paul tells Timothy to feast on the Word and to strive for a godly life. While physical training has its benefits, godliness impacts our entire lives, but it takes training and discipline. Godliness does not just happen, any more than does running a four-minute mile on the first attempt. The word *train*

(4:7) comes from a Greek word that translates into the English as gymnasium or gymnastics. It means the rigorous, strenuous, self-sacrificing training of an athlete.

For believers, the discipline is to be in *godliness*. This word expresses the reality of reverence, piety, and true spiritual virtue. It was a word that was directly connected with worship. Even the pagans used the word *godliness* to mean a concern for the gods and a reverence for those things that are holy.[3]

Discipleship and worship go together; they are not mutually exclusive ideas, but mutually reinforcing realities. The problem that we will face in discipleship is that, if it does not immediately lead us to worship, it then becomes personal edification, which will lead to arrogance, self-righteousness, and self-sufficiency. Likewise, if our worship does not immediately lead us into a disciplined following of Jesus, we might not really be worshiping God at all.

Thus, Paul calls the church to be structured so that believers will not only be disciplers but also worshipers—and worshipers whose worship is expressed through godliness. MacArthur writes:

> Godliness is a right attitude and response toward the true Creator God; a preoccupation from the heart with holy and sacred realities. It is respect for what is due to God, and is thus the highest of all virtues.[4]

And so, in order to impact our world and to be the servants that Christ calls us to be, we strive for biblical godliness, that every day we want to be more like Christ and every day we want to exalt Him as our Savior.

4. The church must be structured to care for and discipline its members. As Paul addressed the need for Pastor Timothy to confront issues within the congregation—and especially with specific offending men and women in the church—he was to do it within a specific challenge. His church was not perfect.

Kent Hughes writes:

> Some of these elders had sinned against their consciences and shipwrecked their faith—men like Hymenaeus, who preached that the resurrection had already taken place, effectively tossing out

the gospel (cf. 1 Timothy 1:19–20; 2 Timothy 2:17–18). "Godless myths" and "genealogies" and "old wives' tales" and "controversies" had become the main fare of these false teachers. Their "gospel" was a deadly, life-denying asceticism (cf. 1 Timothy 1:3–4; 4:1–7).

Adding to the confusion, their female devotees, whom Paul terms "weak-willed women, who are loaded down with sins and are swayed by all kinds of evil desires, always learning but never able to acknowledge the truth" (2 Timothy 3:6–7), had been involved in subverting church order (cf. 1 Timothy 2:8–15). The effect was a whirling chessboard of theological and relational confusion.

The ministry had become increasingly misshapen due to weak management. It was losing its center. The main things, gospel and mission, were becoming increasingly marginalized. Good things like the care of widows were becoming the main things. Timothy was being called to say some hard things. Rebukes were required.[5]

Notice the substance of the entire conversation. It was not unbridled or unloving discipline. It certainly was not self-centered (i.e., I am rebuking you because you hurt my feelings or did not do what I wanted). Rather, this example demonstrates how healthy Christians and a healthy church should look. They are characterized by their love for each other. The foundation of the discussion was that they were brothers and sisters in Christ. Therefore, the church has a structure that allows for believers to have their needs met but also to understand the importance of what it means to be a part of that congregation.

5. The church must be structured to promote healthy relationships. My observation and conclusion on biblical leadership is that the Bible does not really talk so much about leadership the way that many Christian leaders do. If we lead like Jesus, we lead as servants. I may be overstating that supposition, but I have observed too many churches implode because of the prideful attitudes of leaders, both laymen and pastors.

I understand the saying, but I do not fully agree with those who say, "everything rises and falls on leadership"; in the church, everything rises and falls on Jesus and the cross. A careful examination of any church will bear this fact out: healthy churches need healthy leaders and healthy churches need healthy relationships. Here is how Paul describes this attitude and action.

I. Healthy relationships require that we honor our leaders. While Paul looks specifically at the role of the pastor in 5:17–22, take it a little further and apply it to anyone in leadership. While the church is responsible for its pastoral leaders, it is also certainly responsible for honoring all of its leaders. The *double honor* does not reference double pay—as nice as that would be for preachers!—but actually it means "twofold honor," honor shown in two ways: 1) respect and 2) remuneration. This idea is not only correct, it is an ancient interpretation. Fourth-century theologian John Chrysostom said this verse called for reverence and support.[6]

II. Healthy relationships require that we protect our leaders. One of the ways that Satan is attacking the church is by attacking her leaders. I'm not sure if that would be news to anyone, but Satan believes if he can bring down the leader, he can bring down the church.

Look at Paul's advice: *Don't accept an accusation against an elder unless it is supported by two or three witnesses. Publicly rebuke those who sin, so that the rest will also be afraid.* Paul was saying that there were leaders in Ephesus who were worthy of twofold honor because they did their jobs with integrity. Sadly, there were others who were failing.

Therefore, Paul insisted that a high degree of caution is in order because pastoral leadership is a profession that depends on character. If leaders do not maintain character, they can lose everything except salvation. Next to life in Christ, character is the most valuable possession.

Additionally, church leaders are highly vulnerable to the attacks of those who have been hurt previously, who bear ill will toward leadership, or who are offended when they do not get their way. They gossip and call into question the integrity of the leader and, unfortunately, it is human nature to believe the worst in a person. Even John Calvin faced this dilemma. He writes concerning his pastorate in Geneva:

> . . . as soon as any charge is made against ministers of the Word, it is believed as surely and firmly as if it had been already proved. This happens not only because a higher standard of integrity is required from them, but because Satan makes most people, in fact nearly everyone, overcredulous so that without investigation,

they eagerly condemn their pastors whose good name they ought to be defending.[7]

If you know anything about Calvin, he was fired from his pastorate in Geneva over two things: one was the issue of the separation of church and state where Calvin believed that the church should influence the state but the state should not influence the church. The magistrates who were members of his church were unhappy with this stance. Second, people did not like his preaching because it was specific and forceful. Interesting enough, after he was exiled, the ones that fired him begged him to return. He did and then they turned on him again for the same reasons.

III. Healthy relationships require that we be discerning in selecting our leaders. In order to love the church and have a healthy church, we need healthy leaders. And if we do not have standards for what it means to serve, whether as pastoral staff or other positions of leadership in the church, we are not helping them. We are actually doing someone a disservice by moving them into leadership if they are not ready. Paul makes that point in 5:22–25. To be healthy, we need to choose our leaders carefully and structure our churches so that good leaders can be selected.

Structure is far more than whether a church has a plurality of elders who lead the church or whether the church desires to be congregationally governed. Both of these structures work and both have failed miserably. Take note of the spiritual conditions that are necessary in order for a church to function correctly. If these spiritual steps are not followed, the church—regardless of how it was birthed—will probably fall into the trap of control. The church is either structured for growth or is controlled by a few. When control becomes the norm, it is almost certain that a growth plateau is on the horizon.

Control Structures

One of the difficult issues of dealing with power groups in the church is that all of them, even when the pastor or pastors are involved, think that they are helping the church. Every power group considers itself to be the protector and perhaps savior of the congregation. The pastor is no longer effective, and the power group is going to save the church from the pastor's bad decisions, pastoring, preaching, vision, or ladder climbing.

The pastor and his group believe that they are protecting the church from the onset of spiritual hypocrisy and carnality. Rarely does a group admit that their real motive is control. The old saying goes, "If you are not a boss at work or at home, you will be a boss at church."

The other side of the issue is that power is not inherently bad. People in the church will use their influence to move the church into certain directions, and oftentimes that influence can be positive. They want to use their position or reputation to move the church to a deeper discipleship, to a passion for evangelism, or to a love for missions. Those are good motives and should lead the church to growth.

Most power seats in the church, unfortunately, offer a temptation more toward control than influence. When a healthy, spiritual church structure is not in place, these power structures tempt people toward control. When the pastor challenges these groups, it rarely turns out well for him because they see the challenge as an attack on their integrity. Power groups are a prime reason, not only why a church moves into a plateau and into a decline, but also why pastoral tenure becomes shorter and shorter in declining churches. I do not think pastors leave declining churches necessarily because they are in decline. They leave because they get fired, get tired, or get out while they still can. The fight becomes too great a burden, so they leave and go to the next opportunity.

Why the Fight for Control?

When I first started doing research for a class I was teaching at The Southern Baptist Theological Seminary on change and conflict, one of the areas I tried to research was the number of pastors who leave the ministry every year. All of us have heard the "1500 a month" statistic. In some of the statistics I quoted in my book *Can These Bones Live?*, that number was repeated. LifeWay Research Group, however, has updated and corrected those stats. According to them, the original statistic came from an anecdotal question asked at a pastor's conference that took place at Fuller Seminary. The information was never intended to be used as actual research, but it has been communicated as such.

LifeWay researcher Scott McConnell has concluded that pastors are not leaving the ministry in droves. McConnell estimates a total of 29,000 evangelical pastors have left the pastorate over the past decade, an average of fewer than 250 a month.[8] Reasons for pastors leaving the ministry and for their termination are varied. Brooks Faulkner offers these conclusions:

> The most frequently stated reasons for termination revolved around a lack of unity in the congregation. Sixty-six percent stated: A small but powerful minority of members. Forty-one percent stated: Factions in the congregation. Sixteen percent stated: Differed with congregation over leadership style of pastor. Twelve percent stated: Been at church too long. Twelve percent stated: Too authoritarian or dictatorial. Ten percent stated: Couldn't get along with members. Ten percent stated: Not spending enough time on the job.[9]

When we examine the church as a whole, we recognize that evangelicals are planting 3,500 churches a year, but 3,500–4,000 churches are closing.[10] Eighty to eighty-five percent of churches are plateaued or are in decline. Win Arn, in his book *The Pastor's Manual for Effective Ministry*, writes, "Many churches begin a plateau or slow decline about their fifteenth or eighteenth year. Eighty to eighty-five percent are on the down-side of this cycle."[11] In 2005, Thom Rainer agreed with this assessment, writing, "Eight out of ten of the approximately 400,000 churches in the United States are declining or have plateaued."[12] Most recently, Rainer has submitted new research that redirects those earlier findings. He has concluded, in researching 1,000 churches with data available in 2013 and 2016, that 56 percent of churches are declining and 9 percent are plateaued, or a 65 percent rule. While the new research is less discouraging, it still means that two-thirds of our churches are in trouble.[13] In addition to these disturbing statistics, 35 percent of church plants fail by year five.[14]

While a number of reasons can be given for why churches struggle, a major problem within many of our congregations is conflict. When asked why they left their previous church, according to the LifeWay study,

> Most said they moved on because they had taken the previous church as far as they could (54%). However, 23 percent of pastors who changed churches say they left because of conflict in the church. Church conflict often took multiple forms in pastors'

last churches, including significant personal attacks against 34 percent of the pastors.

Pastors also reported conflict over changes they proposed (38%), their leadership style (27%), expectations about the pastor's role (25%), and doctrinal differences (13%). Thirty-eight percent faced conflict with lay leaders, and 31 percent found themselves in conflict with a church matriarch or patriarch. More than a third of pastors (34%) say they left a previous church because their family needed a change. One in five found the church did not embrace their approach to pastoral ministry (19%). Pastors also cited poor fit and unrealistic expectations (18 percent each) as reasons for leaving. Some were reassigned (18%) or asked to leave (8%).[15]

The point is, conflict is real in the church, and if we do not understand why it happens, it will continue in the church. This issue doesn't discriminate based on age; conflict is an issue with new and old congregations alike.

Church Conflict Defined

How do we define conflict in the church? Precise definitions of conflict are difficult to formulate without aspects of delimitation or description. Arnold Kurtz explains:

Synonyms such as "clash," "tension," "struggle," and/or "friction" are usually employed, but they do not stand alone, or are inadequate in themselves, in providing definitions. Is, for instance, the "tension" or "struggle" intra- or inter-personal, intra- or inter-group? And is the "tension" and "struggle" over one or more of the following general areas of conflict: (a) money; (b) power (including authority and structure); (c) value and belief; (d) loyalty to persons and groups?[16]

Conflict may be defined to include any matter that terminates, limits, or prohibits Christians from acting or interacting with one another in a spiritually compelling way and, therefore, affects their ability to serve the Lord according to Scripture. Church conflict in the congregation is "a situation in which two or more members or factions struggle aggressively over what is, or appears to be mutually exclusive beliefs, values, assumed powers or goals."[17] Ken Sande says that "conflict is a difference in opinion or purpose that frustrates someone else's opinion or purpose."[18]

The Reasons for Church Conflict

So why is there conflict in the church? The answers are not simple, and their resolve are even more difficult. The foundation for the inauguration of conflict does, however, have its roots in the biblical text.

The Genesis Account

One needs only to go to the account of Adam and Eve, and subsequently to the encounter of Cain with Abel to find the beginnings of conflict. When Eve listened to Satan in the garden, the Bible says, "The woman saw that the tree was good for food and delightful to look at, and that it was desirable for obtaining wisdom. So she took some of its fruit and ate it; she also gave some to her husband, who was with her, and he ate it" (Gen. 3:6). The result of that action was conflict, both with God and with each other (Gen. 3:8–12).

That conflict led to another that ended in death and the fulfillment of the promise God made to humanity of the consequences of sin. Genesis tells us that Cain and his brother Abel brought offerings to the Lord but that the Lord had regard for Abel's offering but not for Cain's. Cain obviously did not know how to process the now released anger and jealously that he felt and experienced, and as a result, he killed his own brother (Gen. 4:8). The Bible explains to us that all of humanity sins because we are born with this same nature to sin. Scripture says that we are born sinners and that we are by nature sinners. Ephesians 2:2 declares that prior to conversion we are "sons of disobedience" (ESV). Ephesians 2:3 also establishes this thought, explaining that we are all "by nature children of wrath" (ESV). To be a child of wrath indicates that we are separated from God because of sin. If we are all "by nature children of wrath," it can only be because we are all by nature sinners. We discover this same concept in 1 Corinthians 15:22, that says, "in Adam all die," and Romans 5:12

that states, "Therefore, just as sin entered the world through one man, and death through sin, in this way death spread to all people, because all sinned." Thus, we are all sinners by nature, and we are sinners who respond to our nature by sinning.

Because the Spirit and our flesh are still at war with one another, even Christians will continue to sin on this side of glory. Therefore, the reason that churches have conflict is because Christians sin. This reason may sound simplistic, but our battle with sin leads us to make many poor choices and to fall into conflict.

Take a look at the New Testament church, and the battle with conflict becomes a very probable observation. Though not exhaustive, note these ten examples of conflict in the early church:

1. Religious Traditionalism vs. Christ (John 8:1–11)
2. Struggle of Self-Interest vs. Servanthood (Mark 10:35–45)
3. Diversity in Membership and Prejudice (Acts 6:1–3)
4. Partners in Ministry Split over Disagreement (Acts 15:36–40)
5. Personal and Spiritual Immaturity (1 Cor. 3:1–3)
6. Churches Full of Cliques (1 Cor. 1:10–12; 11:17–22)
7. Individual Responses to Issues and Values (Gal. 2:11–12)
8. Prominent Women Could Not Get Along (Phil. 4:2–3)
9. People Treat Rich Believers Better than Poor Believers (James 2:1–9)
10. Self-Will Along with Rebellious Spirit (James 4:1–3)

Thus, it can easily be concluded that conflict is not a recent development within the church. It is an age-old problem. Remember that many of the great men of God were confronted with conflict.

Spiritual Warfare

In addition to our sinful flesh, Paul teaches Christians that we are to be aware of and engaged in spiritual warfare. He gives this challenge:

Finally, be strengthened by the Lord and by his vast strength. Put on the full armor of God so that you can stand against the schemes of the devil. For our struggle is not against flesh and blood, but against the rulers, against the authorities, against the cosmic powers of this darkness, against evil, spiritual forces in the heavens. For this reason take up the full armor of God, so that you may be able to resist in the evil day, and having prepared everything, to take your stand. (Eph. 6:10–13)

The reason that we have conflict in the church is because it is a spiritual battle. Satan's desire is to destroy the church and to destroy believers. One of the most difficult realities I had when I first graduated from seminary and headed off to pastor a church for the first time without the safety net of seminary and friends was this realization: Satan often uses God's own people to do his bidding. I was ready to fight the world, but what I was not ready to do was to deal with conflict in the church. These are God's people, and they are not supposed to act in godless ways. Yet they do because the church is a contended place of spiritual warfare.

Power Struggles

Within the context of sin nature and spiritual warfare comes the issue of power struggles. While we do not wrestle against flesh and blood and we realize that church people are not our enemy, spiritual warfare oftentimes manifests itself in battles over control and leadership.

Carl George, in the book he coauthored with Robert Logan entitled *Leading and Managing Your Church*, presented the idea of a berry-bucket theory, drawing from a practice used by his grandfather in distributing his buckets of berries for consumption. George utilized this idea to categorize those investors in the church who hold claim to the power and future of the church. In this analogy, George identifies two primary groups, with two subgroups under each major grouping. The theory says that the makeup of the church's membership includes people both older and younger than the pastor who were members before the pastor began his service. With these former members, or formerberries, are older and younger people who joined the church after the pastor's tenure commenced, or what he calls newberries.[19]

What I have learned is that, within most churches, five groups of people will be present. While primarily all of the characteristics fit each grouping, exceptions do exist, especially among the ranks of those who are already members of the church. These groupings include:

1. Older Thirties: people who have been members of the church at least thirty years.
2. Younger Thirties
3. Older Tens: people who have been members at least ten years.
4. Younger Tens
5. Newbies: people who have joined the church during the current pastor's tenure.[20]

George calls these individuals "investors" in the church, and that designation is very true. What many pastors and new people fail to realize is the amount of investment people have in their church. Many times, it is a financial investment. They have given the money, built the buildings, and made sacrifices so that the church would survive. Their investment is also in time and service. The church sits where it is because these investors have paid a significant price. New people do not appreciate such nostalgia.

When those things are not appreciated or are threatened, conflict arises. Among the thirties are families who have been in the church a long time. Parents, grandparents, children, and grandchildren all play a part in the stakeholder mentality. Therefore, when their family name or welfare is threatened, people rise up in arms.

This fact is especially true in the small to medium-sized church, along with churches that are more rural than suburban. Interesting enough, many large churches also suffer from this same conundrum. The rural church has traditionally and continues to be driven by family connections. People grew up on the family farm, and the church grew because families grew. Family farms, however, in many areas are disappearing, and children are no longer staying at home. Thom Rainer predicts that a hundred thousand churches are going to close their doors in the next decade, and most of these churches are rural in nature.[21] The problem, though, is much more rooted in the struggle for power than it is in church size or setting. When that power group is threatened, conflict results.

Changes in the Church

Another issue that causes great conflict in churches is the need for change. Usually when a new pastor arrives, he comes with great visions of what the church can become. He immediately sees some of the short-comings of the church, along with having been exposed to churches that are growing rapidly. Therefore, he promptly begins to implement changes that will benefit the church numerically and spiritually.

The problem is, however, everyone resists change. The small to medium-sized church is often criticized for not being willing to change, but that accusation is somewhat misguided. Resistance to change is true regardless of the size of the church. We might assume that the church is small because it has fought change, but there are many large congregations that are also opposed to anything that changes their polity, structure, or relationships. Size does not necessary affirm a church's acceptance of or even need for change.

The reason that many pastors find an unwillingness by people to change is because they fail to examine, communicate, and strategize the need for and process for change. While church stagnation and decline are sources for conflict through change, so is church growth. When churches experience growth, it demands that the church changes in order to structure for the growth and have systems in place to accommodate future growth. Those changes cause conflict.

Just remember this adage: *How many church members does it take to change a lightbulb? Change, what do you mean change?* Change is possible, but change usually takes a lot of time and a lot of preparation.

Cultural Differences

Within the context of change, there are times that a pastor seeks to bring about a change merely due to cultural preferences rather than real need. Culture is a source of conflict within the church. Culture applies to polity, preferences, and personalities. In the realm of polity, churches behave the way they do or follow the particular procedures they do because is it a part of their cultural norm. Churches develop habits that lead to policy and procedure. Christians form certain biases or convictions based upon their upbringing or in reaction to perceived or real abuses. For example, for some Christians, it is accounted as sin to bring food or drink into the area called the sanctuary or worship center. They have been taught that this area is sacred. When newcomers or teenagers show up with sodas in their hands, it becomes a real source of conflict.

Conflict arises out of preference. Every Christian likes a certain style of music, worship, teaching, preaching, polity, order, and method. Oftentimes these methods are equated with Scripture. For instance, many churches conduct the same style of evangelistic outreach that they did twenty years ago, not because it is effective, but because they believe that the church would be accused of being non-evangelistic if they did not do it. If someone tries to change that methodology, accusations and suspicions begin.

Culture creates conflict when the culture of the church becomes significantly different from the culture of the community. This issue is not just a white or Caucasian issue; it is a factor that affects people of all colors and races. When the neighborhood begins to change from being a neighborhood that defines a different racial or cultural makeup, the church must decide if it will embrace the new culture or reject it. Regardless of the decision, conflict results. In small and medium-sized churches, these cultural differences are far more noticeable than in the larger church. Add one white person to a choir of a thousand Asian-Americans and no one notices. Add one white person to a choir of ten, and the picture becomes quite clear. The church either welcomes and celebrates the cultural change, or conflict ensues.

Internal Conflicts

An interesting development within the church has been the creation of entities whose primary purpose is peacemaking among Christians. While some may accuse these entrepreneurs of exploiting a delicate situation, their rise demonstrates the level of conflict that has arisen in the church and the fact that churches, in the past, have not adequately dealt with the issue, especially as it relates to internal conflicts between believers. One such group is the Institute for Christian Conciliation. They list six reasons for conflict. The following is an adaptation of their findings:

1. Intrapersonal Conflicts—This type of conflict is within one's self, such as anger or bitterness.
   Spiritual warfare—moral, ethical, spiritual low
   Family—marriage conflict, family unsupportive, health issues
   Calling conflict—am I in the wrong ministry area?
   Ministry/church conflict—do I need to be here?

2. Substantive/Strategic Conflicts—Examples of this type of conflict are church budgets, committees, removal of pastor or other church staff, members, church building projects.
3. Value and Belief Conflicts—This type of conflict deals with Bible doctrine.
4. Relationship/Interpersonal Conflicts—This type of conflict deals with the heart in the area of lack of forgiveness and making things right with an individual or a group.
5. Information Conflicts—The way information is given out to staff or the church on any issue.
6. System/Structural Conflicts—This type of conflict is how a church is governed, organized, and who is responsible for what.[22]

While some of their findings are overlapping with other findings already mentioned in this paper, it is clear that much of the fault of conflict within the church finds its root in internal issues, not in external ones. While many pastors cite attacks on the church by the world, the real problem is far more internal than external.

Making Application to Church/Personal Conflicts

In addition to all these factors mentioned, there are myriad other factors involved in church conflict. We must turn now to consider how we can resolve and move forward in the midst of these conflicts. A study of conflict would not be complete without at least a call for and process for reconciliation. How does the church or individuals within the church resolve conflicts?

Conflict Between Individuals

First, start by developing the right attitude and heart. This first step is the most difficult step because it involves the following characteristics:

- Meekness (Gal. 6:1)
- Humility (James 4:10)
- Forgiveness (Eph. 4:31–32)
- Patience (James 1:19–20)

Second, lead the church and the offending/offended parties to evaluate their part(s) in the conflict. Adrian Rogers once said, "It's got to be an awfully flat pancake to have only one side."[23] While the offending/offended parties often believe it is always the other person's fault, rarely is it one-sided. Consider this passage of Scripture:

Matthew 7:1–5—remove the log from your own eye first

Third, lead the offended party to the individual (not to others) to voice their concern, with the goals of reconciliation, forgiveness, and restoration. Examine these two passages:

2 Corinthians 5:16–21—the ministry of reconciliation

Matthew 18:15—you have won your brother

Fourth, remind those involved to look to others within the church, and especially in leadership, to help with mediation. Consider this passage:

"But if he won't listen, take one or two others with you, so that by the testimony of two or three witnesses every fact may be established." (Matt. 18:16)

Finally, be committed to the task that, if the person refuses to reconcile, church leadership needs to determine the next step. Ask these two questions:

Is this an offense of sin that needs to go before the church?

Is it simply a matter that the two can "agree to disagree" but can walk together as friends?[24]

Church Conflict

In addition to the principles that apply to conflict between individuals, one must consider conflict within the larger context of the congregation, how conflict flows out from individuals and affects the corporate body, and how one must deal with that level of conflict. Note these ideas:

1. Fortify your prayer life.
2. Engage in spiritual warfare.

3. Seek prayer support, accountability, and mentorship from a trusted fellow pastor or denominational leader.
4. Establish a practical strategy to resolve the conflict. Realize that time is of the essence.
5. Involve the appropriate leadership group in the church.
6. Request consultation from another pastor or denominational leader to provide guidance for the leadership group.
7. If specialized help is needed, call upon others outside of the church to help.[25]

Conflict Prevention

Wisdom teaches us to seek to prevent conflict before it starts. While some conflict is inevitable, especially when dealing with sinful people, some of it can be avoided or at least somewhat neutralized. Here is a short list of possible ideas:

1. *Work with the leaders of the church.* Remember that the tribal chief, older/younger thirties have considerable influence in the church. Avoid the temptation of running over the leaders or assuming that they are not spiritual simply because they disagree with the pastor's desires or goals. Remember that they have seen pastors come and go and have heard all of the grand goals with no result. Be patient to work with them and to gain their trust.
2. *Orchestrate change carefully.* Determine which changes are triage changes and which changes are secondary. Conflict happens because new ideas often clash with old structures. Therefore, demonstrate care in bringing about changes that minimize the threat to the congregation.
3. *Maintain communication.* Pastors often assume that people hear and understand the goals and direction of the church. Note this standard of communicating vision: When the vision caster is absolutely tired of communicating to the church the vision, it is then that the church is just beginning to hear it. Do not make the mistake of implementing the "need to know" adage. Communication is essential in the small to medium-sized church.[26]

Pastors need to embrace the fact that conflict is inevitable in the church. Churches have problems because people have problems. Churches have problems because they still deal with the issue of the fallen nature of humanity. People are sinners by nature, and they respond to that nature by choosing to sin.

> Churches have problems because people have problems.

Conflict in the church, though, does not necessarily have to be destructive. Many of those within the church reconciliatory ministry say that conflict is essentially neutral. When handled properly, it can result in some positive benefits for the church. Consider these possible outcomes of conflict:

- It can serve as a stimulus that stirs new ideas and processes for decision-making.
- It can help people distinguish better between two points of view.
- It can help a church better define its identity or beliefs.
- It can help hasten change.
- It can stimulate productive dialogue and build new relationships.
- It can encourage a healthy reexamination of assumptions and preconceptions.
- It can lead to the discovery of new ideas, approaches, and methods.
- It can stimulate personal growth.

Conflict, on the other hand, becomes detrimental when it is not handled correctly or when it remains unchecked and finds its source deep within the sinful nature and motives of people. Ken Sande writes, "It can lead to alienation, anger, pain, humiliation, defensiveness, physical illness, and can lead to broken families, friendships, and businesses, and drastically diminish the witness and outreach of the church."[27]

Eric Reed echoes much of this sentiment through a survey of 506 pastors conducted by *Leadership*. They responded by saying of the negative outcomes of conflict:

- Damaged relationships: 68%
- Sadness: 58%
- Decline in attendance: 32%

- Leaders left the church: 32%
- Loss of trust: 31%
- Bitterness: 29%
- Loss of communication with congregation: 3%[28]

Therefore, when conflict is something that causes or could cause destruction or decline, it must be addressed and nullified. Conflict is not the end of the church, but it certainly will facilitate a church's death if left unchecked and allowed to fester.

Finally, conflict is not necessarily a characteristic of the small or medium-sized church alone. There are churches within these size ranges that are healthy and growing. There are also large and megachurches that are overwhelmed with conflict and are now on the decline or have even ceased to exist. Thus, the Scripture gives an excellent challenge and reminder regardless of the size church that we serve, "Be sober-minded, be alert. Your adversary the devil is prowling around like a roaring lion, looking for anyone he can devour" (1 Pet. 5:8).

Structure or Control?

If a church does not plan ahead, always moving and developing a growth structure, it most probably will experience battles for control. In fact, the evidences of those battles for control have already begun, even while the church is still in its younger stages. Conflict, being a part of our sin nature, becomes an easy consequence when the church misaligns its structure. Churches that continue up their growth plane have usually developed a structure that curbs the power appeal.

I have taught and preached this thought numerous times: Satan uses God's own people to do his bidding. Poor structure in a church serves as a conduit for Satan's devices against the church. When God's people fight, everyone loses. Therefore, work together as a church to develop a healthy church with a healthy leadership that leads through a healthy structure.

The Stages of Decline

CHAPTER 5

Plateau

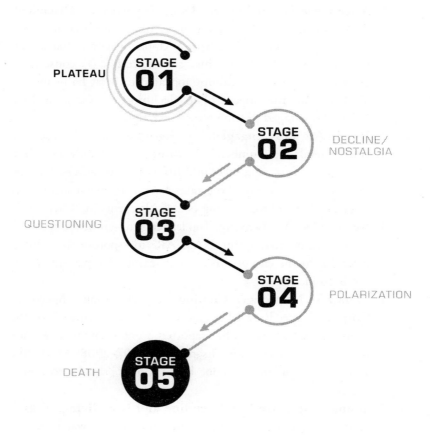

B rian Dodd offers an interesting perspective on why churches are
plateauing or declining, drawing from a report that *USA Today* did

on the declining attendance at NASCAR events and using these similarities as a springboard for discussion, debate, and reversing the trends. (I recently watched the Brickyard 400, and so many of these observations were evident in just this one race.) He writes:

The following are just **13 Reasons Churches Have Plateaued or Declining Attendance** I gleaned from the article:

1. **Attendance Is No Longer Being Reported or Discussed.** When a church tells you its membership rather than its attendance, you are in trouble. Bristol Motor Speedway has a seating capacity of 146,000. This venue once had 55 consecutive sellouts. In 2016, the stadium appeared to be at half-capacity. To hide the true impact of its declining numbers, in 2012 NASCAR stopped posting attendance figures.

2. **People Are Less Engaged.** Are you tracking and discussing your attendance numbers? According to MediaWatch.com, seven of the first eight races in 2016 had lower ratings than the previous year. Four of those races had their lowest ratings yet since Fox began broadcasting NASCAR events in 2001.

3. **Key Leaders Are Leaving.** Top leaders will not be reduced to a level of mediocrity. Sprint, NASCAR's top sponsor since 2004, is leaving at the end of this current season. A replacement has not been identified.

4. **Money Is No Longer Coming In.** International Speedway Corp. and Speedway Motorsports Inc., which run 20 of the sport's 23 racing tracks, has reported event attendance revenue is down 49 percent from its peak in 2007–2008. Much like a church, attendance revenue is the sport's primary economic engine.

5. **Young People Are Not Attending and Not Giving.** Today's young people have multiple opportunities to watch racing other than onsite attendance. However, NASCAR is struggling how to monetize online viewership. This is a similar problem churches now face. Driver Brad Keselowski said, "It is easier than ever to get access to different platforms without attending.

That is a lot of how the sport is monetized, through actual attendance."

6. **Your Core Audience Feels Neglected.** Constant changes in your ministry focus causes a loss of trust. Similarly, NASCAR fan Lanette Williams said, "The constant changes NASCAR does, it doesn't have the same good feeling it used to have. We lost interest in NASCAR. NASCAR has lost interest in us."

7. **Your Audience Has Grown Old.** Successful organizations are green and growing. In other words, there is a continual pipeline of young talent being groomed for future leadership. Fox Sports 1 had the highest cable rating for adults 50 and over for a recent race at Michigan International Speedway. Conversely, the same race was tied for fourth in the age 18–49 category. NASCAR is not green and growing. It is brown and declining.

8. **Your Audience Has No Sense of Expectation.** Your people are bored. You see it in their eyes during church services. They are glassed over. Their body language is lifeless. And worse, they do not invite their friends to church. But people who have a great worship experience will likely return and bring others. NASCAR COO Brent Dewar said, "A fan that attends a live event is an absolute keystone of the sport for us. If the experience is awesome and they have all the amenities they want, all of our research points to the fact you have a chance to make a fan for life."

9. **You Are Losing Key Staff.** Some NASCAR officials are pointing to the loss of Jeff Gordon to retirement and Tony Stewart to injury as a cause for the sport's attendance decline.

10. **You Have a Weak Leadership Team.** John Maxwell said, "Those closest to the leader determine the success of the leader." Texas Motor Speedway President Eddie Gossage says, "No one driver is going to sell you tickets, and no one driver is going to put you out of business. Each driver represents a slice of the pie that makes up the whole." It takes a team.

11. **You Are Trying to Redefine Success.** Instead of making the hard choices to make your ministry relevant again, you talk about how deep your people are and your grand vision for the

future. You take the easy way out by praying for "revival." Then after unsuccessfully praying for revival, you blame a lukewarm age and say, "Well, God just didn't bless." Instead of NASCAR talking about how to increase raceway attendance, merchandise sales, and television viewers, some executives are now attempting to change the conversation to social engagement, followers, exposures, and impressions. But Just Marketing International's Zak Brown brings a word of caution. He says, "Digital is how the world is consuming everything but digital is still new. I don't think anyone has figured out how to quantify digital exposure yet."

12. **You Have Started Forming Committees.** NASCAR calls it collaboration. But in an attempt to garner young viewers, they have formed a driver's council, a manufacturer's council, an owner's alliance, and now a track council. Sound like your church?

13. **You No Longer Focus on the Bottom Line.** You do not count what counts. The article concludes with Brown bringing everyone back to the bottom line. He says, "As long as the needle is moving on their (sponsors') business, that's ultimately their No. 1 measurement. Measuring eyeballs and attendance is less than, 'Did I sell more cans of Coke? Did I sell more Subway sandwiches?' As long as those metrics say, 'I sold more because of my NASCAR sponsorship,' that becomes priority No. 1." Your church's No. 1 priority should be glorifying Jesus and delivering the type of ministry needed to reach as many people for Him as possible. To begin seeing growth in your church, keep the conversation there.[1]

It seems that the issue of decline is not just a church issue. In many cases, it is a cultural issue. For example, retail stores that were late in getting into the online market are rapidly declining during this decade. Derek Thompson reports that this phenomenon is simply because people are doing more retail shopping online that in years past. He asserts:

The simplest explanation for the demise of brick-and-mortar shops is that Amazon is eating retail. Between 2010 and last year

[2016], Amazon's sales in North America quintupled from $16 billion to $80 billion. Sears' revenue last year was about $22 billion, so you could say Amazon has grown by three Sears in six years. Even more remarkable, according to several reports, half of all U.S. households are now Amazon Prime subscribers.[2]

While I do not want to make too close of a comparison, there are some striking similarities. Churches and businesses that embrace change and develop ministries (churches) and market strategies (businesses) that engage these changing landscapes are reaching their target groups. Those who are living in the past and are holding onto past strategies and marketing plans are plateaued and are in decline. Unfortunately, many churches and companies find comfort in the plateau. The problem is that churches and companies do not stay on the plateau. They either retool and revive or they begin to decline. Throughout small-town America, the mom-and-pop retail storefronts are nearly extinct. They could not compete with the megastore that moved into town. When Wal-Mart can sell at retail the same television cheaper than what mom-and-pop can purchase it wholesale, it is not long until consumers, regardless of loyalties, head to the big box store. Churches are in competition with each other but also with so many things in the world. Sunday is no longer the day when everything but the church closes (Chick-fil-A being a notable exception). In one town where I pastored, even the local Christian high school had football practices and other activities on Sunday.

Ten Warning Signs of Plateau

The Malphurs Group has developed a concise list that may provide assistance in helping plateaued churches recognize more responsibly the dangerous position of church plateau. Aubrey Malphurs gives these ten warning signs of a church plateau and some helpful suggestions for dealing with each:

1. **Volunteer numbers have decreased or stalled.** Do you have fewer volunteers actively serving now than three months ago? If so, it may be time to focus on volunteer mobilization and recruitment. Don't know how to recruit more volunteers? Does it feel

like everyone already does too much? Try creating some new volunteer opportunities or train those who are currently serving in how to oversee groups of volunteers.

2. **You spend your time putting out fires rather than planning for growth.** Most people struggle to quantify this one. But on average, how much of your time do you spend planning versus putting out fires? Look for a general tone of tyranny of the urgent vs. careful thinking about ministry direction.

3. **Staff are leaving and not developing.** How long has it been since one of your staff members left? Do you develop your staff? Do your staff members develop and train volunteers? For the overwhelming majority of churches, adding more and more staff members will not sustain the ministry. Consider how leadership development and leadership coaching play into your plan to build into yourself and your staff. If you can develop your staff and train them to develop your volunteers, your ministry will be positioned very well for growth.

4. **Facility issues are disregarded to handle urgent shortfalls.** Have you noticed a few cracks in the wall in one of your buildings? Does your facility need some additional TLC? I find this warning sign over and over as I work with pastors and churches. A rundown facility often indicates a church or ministry that has plateaued, is in decline, or may soon begin to hit a church plateau.

5. **The church's vision looks back more than it looks forward.** When you talk about vision, do you primarily remind people of the past? Or do you paint a picture of a future that they haven't yet experienced? I encourage you to always remember and thank God for what He has done. But don't let gratitude for the past usurp future vision clarity.

6. **The church's core values are more aspirational than actual.** Very, very few churches can truthfully say that all their values manifest as actual core values. For that matter, very few individuals or families can either.

Do your core values reflect your present identity or what you aspire to become? A core value of evangelism comes to mind when I think of aspirational values. Many churches claim to value evangelism, but few of their main leaders shared their faith in the last year. I would call this an aspirational value.

Don't use this warning sign as an excuse to judge or criticize others. We all have values that are more actual and others that are more aspirational. As we help church leadership teams clarify their actual and aspirational values, we see excitement among the leadership as they uncover new areas of focus.

7. **Young families seem to flock to another nearby church.** This painful warning light happens all the time. If you find yourself thinking, "Why do all the young families go to that church?" then this warning sign likely applies to you.

When churches complete our church ministry analysis, I love seeing the impact of clarity on the group's thinking. I recently worked with the church where almost 100 percent of the leadership team indicated that they needed to do a better job with young adults and young families. After I processed the data and presented it to them, everyone in the room shook their heads with an emphatic "YES." If your church avoids this warning light, it could have disastrous long-term effects on the viability of your ministry.

8. **Evaluation considered something that might happen in the future.** When your church focuses primarily on survival, evaluation gets pushed aside. It kills me to see this happen. Evaluation and debriefing create a culture of excellence, because ministry quality gets the attention it deserves.

9. **The concept of small groups doesn't usually extend beyond "Sunday school."** I believe that God is using thousands of Sunday school classes all over the world. So please don't hear me saying that I think we should eliminate Sunday school. That's not what I'm saying at all.

But if the only context for community, spiritual growth, and service is through your Sunday morning Sunday school classes, you may need to reassess your approach to community, discipleship, and service. Small groups held outside of Sunday mornings create an additional context for spiritual growth. They create a

context for guest assimilation. They make a church that is growing a place that continues to feel like a family.

10. **Guests attend, but often do not stay.** Do you wonder why your
guests continue to visit, but don't stick around? Plateaued churches
battle this reality week in and week out. Set up a first impressions
ministry that directly addresses guest assimilation. If you don't
get yourself in the mind of a guest, your on-boarding process will
likely discourage them from deepening their involvement.[3]

The Critical Juncture

The plateau is the critical juncture for the church. If the church does
not recognize its Life Stage, it will soon move away from its plateau and
onto a death plane. Churches that are growing have an upward momentum. Churches on the decline have a downward momentum. Momentum
is like pushing a boulder across a series of hills. Once momentum is
gained and the rock is moving downhill, it is almost impossible to stop
it. It will roll over anyone who gets in the way, but once that momentum
stops, it is almost impossible to get it moving again. It is like pushing
that boulder up a steep hill, lacking the energy and inertia to do so. The
top of the hill seems to get higher, while the energy to push the rock is
obviously diminishing.

The real problem of the idea of plateau is that the term is somewhat
ambiguous and even misleading for the church. Webster's dictionary
defines *plateau* as "to reach a period or phase of stability: level off."[4] A quick
glance at the characteristics that lead to a church plateauing easily debunks
the first part of the definition. Churches that plateau are not at a point of
stability—not unless they are at a moment where they are retooling and
re-visioning for growth again, and even then, that leveling off is certainly
temporary. In the church world, when a church is described as having
plateaued, it usually means that the last five years of statistics have been
examined and that the church has not made any progress numerically.[5]

If this plateau is an anomaly, the church can and probably will
remedy the problem. If the plateau is due to the age of the church or
its changing demographics, the church has to decide its next steps. Jeff
Christopherson believes that every church has a life cycle that eventually

ends. He agrees with the presumption that churches, like organisms, grow fastest at the earliest stages of life and that they are designed to reproduce soon and often. He moves to a sobering thought:

> Finally, like other organisms, ***churches are not intended to continuously grow forever***. They grow fastest in the earliest stages, reproduce frequently during their maturing years and hopefully assist as wise, generous and loving grandparents during their final years.

John Worcester said it's tragic "that most churches do just the opposite to what they are intended to do. When they start to plateau, rather than to ramp up reproduction, they turn inward and concentrate on their own growth. Churches choose birth control and the exponential advance of the Kingdom ceases."

Which leads us back to our problem. With 70 percent of our churches in a state of plateau or decline, what are the options?

Celebrate Well. Remember all the ways God has used this church to expand His Kingdom. Recall the faces and families that have been unmistakably impacted by the faithfulness of this church. Perhaps remembering the past will serve as a re-tracking for the future. Revelation 2:5 instructs us to remember and repeat the earlier things.

Remember Kingdom. No cold cup of water offered humbly in Jesus' name is without eternal impact. Think of how King Jesus might use the resources and wisdom that He has blessed you with for increased Kingdom impact. The lore of church growth tells us that we are corporate failures if we are unable to produce winning numbers. The King of the Kingdom tells us that true Kingdom fruit is found in an openhanded posture of selflessness. "Truly, truly, I say to you, unless a grain of wheat falls into the earth and dies, it remains alone; but if it dies, it bears much fruit" (John 12:24 ESV).

Think Multiplication. How might you bear much fruit? Certainly not by going down grasping clenched-fisted as a dead-end link on the Great Commission chain. We never bear fruit by "saving ourselves." It emerges simply through the spiritual abandonment of "losing ourselves." What about your legacy of multiplication? It is the assignment to which God has called His church.

Do healthy churches continually grow? The evidence for our first 2000 years would lead us to an unequivocal "No." Does "plateaued or declining" mean little Kingdom impact? It all depends on Whose church it is.[6]

The good news is that there are exceptions to even this rule of thumb. Churches live and die, but they can continue to thrive even beyond their expected expiration date. Take note of this testimony by Chris Hefner:

On October 5, [2014], Mud Creek Baptist Church celebrated its 211th anniversary. The church has a unique history. Around 1880 the church experienced some major struggles and even considered disbanding. But Betsy Barnett walked from Greenville, SC to Hendersonville, NC (about a 40-mile trip) to vote against disbanding. Solid and stable leadership has exemplified the church since the middle of the twentieth century with only three senior pastors since the 1951. In 1979 the church experienced a tragedy with their pastor for eighteen years, Frank Carter, dying in a car accident. To that point in our church history, Mud Creek was an average Southern Baptist Church in the Bible Belt. Even after stable leadership through the majority of the twentieth century, the church was averaging around 125 people in regular attendance when Greg Mathis was called to be the pastor in 1980.

He has led a Revitalization effort that has spanned his ministry of 34 years at Mud Creek. By every measurable category, the church has grown exponentially. Currently we have around 4,000 members with an average Sunday morning attendance around 2,400 people. We continue to expand numerically, grow in depth within the congregation, and have advanced our missions and outreach partnerships significantly over the last 15 years. Mud Creek is not a perfect church, nor are we healthy by every rubric that could be used. But we do represent almost 2 percent of the population of our county in Sunday morning attendance and continue to reach people with the gospel.[7]

What Is a Church to Do?

When a church hits the proverbial plateau wall, what is it to do? Hefner provides these replicable ideas:

1. Commitment to evangelism and discipleship
2. Leading with people not over them
3. Longevity in leadership
4. Willingness to adapt
5. Consistent vision casting and outward emphasis
6. Positive, worshipful atmosphere
7. Regard for heritage without being tied down by tradition
8. Dependence on God but not pharisaical super spirituality[8]

While churches do die, there are scores of churches that have weathered the storms of time and have the potential to grow again. The years of plateau and even decline can be a positive situation in the life of the church as it now has time to re-vision itself for the future, to experience a rebirth of sorts.

Thom Rainer provides some additional help at this point. In an article he wrote on church revitalization, he mentioned eight common characteristics that took place in the congregations he researched that had gone through revitalization without changing their name. Rainer noted that this method is not the most effective but it worked in these cases. He advised that the key factor was that leaders were willing to make the sacrifices necessary to see their church revitalize. Remember that one detail: Sacrifice is the key dynamic.

Rainer reports:

1. **The pastor formed an alliance of key influencers in the church.** This group is not informal, nor is it closed to others. It begins when the pastor identifies those in the church whose voices are most effective in leading others toward change. I cannot remember a revitalization effort that succeeded without an alliance.

2. **The alliance of influencers recognized the need for church revitalization and made a commitment to pray for it daily.** Please don't let the last part of the preceding sentence escape your notice. Each of the influencers committed to daily prayer

for revitalization. They realized it could not take place in their power alone.

3. **The leaders and a growing number in the congregation made a commitment to move the church to look more like the community.** Such a commitment naturally involves an outward focus, because declining churches are not reaching all segments of their communities. The leadership within the church begins to look at the demographics of their community. They are willing to face reality on where the church is falling short.

4. **The church began to confront the issue of sacred cows.** I know of one church that had a two-hour "town hall" meeting of the members of the congregation. The leaders made a list of every preference and church activity they could recall. For example, one of the items on the list was "11 a.m. worship." They then labeled each activity as either biblically essential, contextual, or traditional.

5. **The leadership began to work with the congregation to form a clear and compelling vision.** One church, an all Anglo congregation, cast a vision to have 20 percent Hispanics in the worship attendance in one year because the community was 40 percent Hispanic. They did not reach 20 percent in year one, but they did in year two.

6. **The leadership communicated a sense of urgency.** One of the simplest yet most powerful communications of urgency I've heard is: We change or we die. Too many congregations are choosing to die because of their unwillingness to change.

7. **The leadership, particularly the pastor, was willing to endure a season of intense criticism.** This point is often where revitalization efforts end. The critics can get nasty, and the criticisms can become intense. Many people simply get mad at the idea of change.

8. **The leadership of the church was willing to let go of members.** I have never known a successful revitalization effort where members did not leave. Few leaders like to see members leave, but some churches have a "back door revival" before true revitalization can take place.[9]

Thus, there is hope, even for a church that is older, is in a changing neighborhood, or is in a plateaued town or location. Take note of both the statistics and the attitude of the church and use them to lead the church to see the need to start growing again. While the church is a living organism, it is different in one particular area. An organism is an entity within itself; the church, however, is a changing organism. New is always available. Rebirth is always possible. When new people come into a church, it demonstrates that the church can start anew.

Change Is on the Horizon

The church on the plateau is actually in a good spot to get back on the growth plane. The church has settled into programs, ministries, and a lifestyle that either are productive or are a hindrance. The ministry "sacred cows" will be difficult to address and eliminate, but if the church recognizes its dilemma, it can overcome.

Pastors must remember that every church has to change and revitalize. Let me give you my definition of revitalization. Revitalization is not a destination. Take note of that fact. People will ask, "How do we know that we have revitalized?" Revitalization is too fluid for a destination. Here is my definition: *Revitalization is the process by which the church learns to embrace the changes necessary to get it back on and keep it on a growth plane.* No, the definition is nothing profound, and anyone can wordsmith it to death. The key thoughts, though, are these:

> Pastors must remember that every church has to change and revitalize.

- Revitalization is a process, not a destination.
- Revitalization helps churches embrace change
- Revitalization gets churches on a growth plane.

The initial indication that a church is on a growth plane is obviously numerical. Numerical growth is important. Growth can also be measured in terms of spiritual maturity and community transformation. We must not determine a church's potential or even success just by whether or not it reaches some arbitrary mark in attendance. We must move away from the terminology and mind-set of the small church, and recognize that 90 percent of our churches have fewer than 299 in gathered worship, 83 percent have fewer than 199, and 63 percent have fewer than 100.[10] In fact, a church that is large in numbers may be unhealthy in many other areas. Therefore, getting a church on a growth plane is far more than just numerical growth.

Even healthy churches reach the point that they need to begin to rethink and revisit their mission and vision. Dale Burke, pastor of First Evangelical Free Church of Fullerton, California, offers this observation about his becoming pastor of the church: "The overall health of the church was my greatest joy as I began to lead. Yet I soon discovered that our *health*—the fact that we did so many things *well*—was also one of my greatest challenges. You see, healthy churches often fail to *feel the need* for change."[11] Burke then offers some helpful reasons why even healthy churches need change:

1. Our world is constantly changing.
2. Our mission is yet to be accomplished.
3. Our people are constantly changing. The majority of churches in America are plateaued or dying for one of two reasons: 1) They change what they should never change, or 2) they refuse to change what they are free to change.
4. Scripture gives us function but not forms.
5. Change is easier when you are healthy, not unhealthy.
6. Creativity should always flow from the children of the Creator.
7. Every ministry has a natural life cycle and will eventually die unless it is reborn from within.[12]

The point is, every church needs to learn to embrace the changes necessary to get it back on and keep it on a growth plane. That statement includes healthy churches, unhealthy churches, and everyone in between. A critical time to make that decision is when the church is at its plateau. If the church does not embrace change, it will begin to slide down the slope toward death.

CHAPTER 6

The Death Spiral

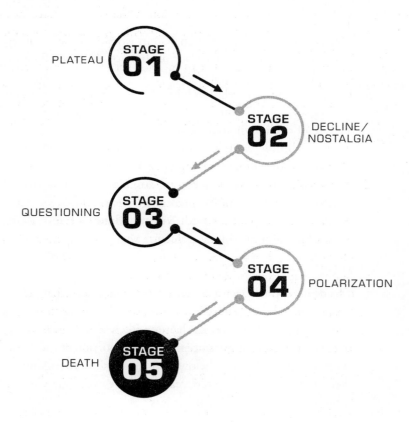

I am not going to spend a great deal of time on the final stages of decline since these stages are addressed in a multitude of sources, but I will utilize these ideas to assist in identifying a church's current status and helping the church get back onto a growth plane. Once a church rolls off the plateau, death is certain unless strategic measures are put into place.

I quoted earlier Thom Rainer's research of one thousand churches in 2013 and 2016. From that data, he updated the percentage of churches that are actually plateaued or are declining. He also offered some sobering discoveries.

1. More than 61 percent of churches average fewer than 100 in worship attendance.
2. Churches that have fewer than 100 in worship are most likely to be declining churches. Two out of three of these small churches are declining.
3. There is a direct correlation with the rate of decline in a church and the size of the church. The smaller the church, the greater the rate of decline in attendance:
   • A declining church with an attendance of 200 or more declines at a rate of 4 percent each year.
   • A declining church with an attendance of less than 100 declines at a rate of 7.6 percent per year.
   • A declining church with an attendance of less than 50 declines at a rate of 8.7 percent a year.

Rainer concluded by saying,

4. It's a death spiral. Declining smaller churches decline much more rapidly than larger churches. Once the declining church goes below 100 in attendance, its days are likely numbered.
5. Here is the sad summary statement of this portion of the research: Once a church declines below 100 in worship attendance, it is likely to die within just a few years. The life expectancy for many of these churches is ten years or less.[1]

Many writers utilize Robert Dale's book *To Dream Again* as a launching pad for describing the downward spiral of a declining church. Though originally published in 1981, his bell curve of decline is still valid and worth studying.

Unfortunately, the reason the downward spiral needs to be addressed and studied is because it is at this point that most new pastors come to a church. Examine the research. Growing churches have pastors with longer tenures; therefore, fewer of those churches have open pulpits. More than half of existing churches are declining. Very few—only 9 percent—are actually plateaued. Thus, most pastors—probably young pastors first entering the ministry, graduating from seminary, or taking their first lead pastor role—are going to take on the responsibility of a revitalization pastor.

The Declining Church Outlook

Churches that find themselves on the downward slope of their life stage go through huge emotion swings. Instead of worship experiences and meetings filled with celebration, they find themselves trying to solve problems. Dale's book can be summarized in this one statement: Growing churches dream dreams and plan; unhealthy/stagnant churches solve problems.[2] It is not that growing churches do not have problems; they do. The problems, however, are not seen as obstacles, but as either growing pains or opportunities for the next stage of growth. Stagnant/declining churches have lost their dream and their focus. Therefore, problems become the primary motivation for existence: how to pay the electric bill, what to do about the empty classrooms, voting to change the nursery into a parlor, cutting the budget, or laying off personnel. One can see how the church falls into a death spiral and why Dale admonishes churches that they must dream again.

Even Businesses Have a Life Cycle

An interesting part of gathering research for this book was the fact that I came across, on a number of occasions, a business bell curve developed by Ichak Adizes.[3]

In the book, he demonstrates, though I would assume unintentionally, how churches and businesses experience comparable emotions and responses to decline. Consider the similarities:

- The Fall/The Plateau
- Aristocracy/Decline-Nostalgia
- Recrimination/Questioning

- Bureaucracy/Polarization
- Death/Death

On his website, Adizes introduces the concept of a corporate lifecycle and the actual need and ability for companies to take an online Lifecycle Assessment. Adizes explains:

At the foundation of effective management for any organization is the fundamental truth that all organizations, like all living organisms, have a lifecycle and undergo very predictable and repetitive patterns of behavior as they grow and develop. At each new stage of development an organization is faced with a unique set of challenges. How well or poorly management addresses these challenges, and leads a healthy transition from one stage to the next, has a significant impact on the success or failure of their organization.

Leading an organization through lifecycle transitions is not easy, or obvious. The same methods that produce success in one stage can create failure in the next. Fundamental changes in leadership and management are all required, with an approach that delicately balances the amount of control and flexibility needed for each stage. Leaders who fail to understand what is needed (and not needed) can inhibit the development of their companies or plunge them into premature aging.

The challenges that every organization must overcome at each stage of development first manifest themselves as problems that arise from the growth and success of the company and from external changes in markets, competitors, technology and the general business and political environment. This simple, unavoidable reality leads to the following five important insights about the nature of problems in organizations.

1. Problems are normal and desirable. Problems are the natural result of change. The only place on the lifecycle curve where there are no problems is the place where there is no change, which is Death.

2. Your role as a leader is not to prevent problems or slow the pace of change. Instead, focus on accelerating your organization's ability to recognize and resolve problems.

3. Some of the problems you face are normal and some are abnormal. Normal problems are those that are expected for a given lifecycle stage. Abnormal problems are those that are not expected (or desirable) in a stage of the lifecycle. Since you will never have enough time or resources to address all the problems you face, focus on abnormal problems. Many normal problems can be ignored since they tend to resolve themselves during the natural course of growth and development.

4. You can drive your organization faster when you know the road ahead. Most of the issues you face are common to all organizations. There is no need for you to reinvent the wheel. You can save a lot of time and effort by thoroughly understanding the nature of all 10 stages in the lifecycle, and knowing what it takes to transition from one stage to the next.

5. Prime is the Fountain of Youth for organizations. One key difference between the lifecycle for human beings versus organizations is that living things inevitably die, while organizations need not. The "age" of a company in terms of its lifecycle is not related to its chronological age, the number of employees, or the size of its assets. Instead, the lifecycle age is defined by the interrelationship between flexibility and control. An organization that is in Prime has achieved a balance between control and flexibility. A Prime organization knows what it is doing, where it is going, and how it will get there. It also enjoys both high growth and high profitability. Once an organization reaches Prime, leadership must work to sustain that position.[4]

Take note of what Adizes says about the difference between the human lifecycle and an organization's lifecycle:

One key difference between the lifecycle for human beings versus organizations is that living things inevitably die, while organizations need not. The "age" of a company in terms of its lifecycle is not related to its chronological age, the number of employees, or the size of its assets. Instead, the lifecycle age is defined by the interrelationship between flexibility and control.[5]

If this statement is true for organizations, how much more is it true for the church? I want to take care at this point, because I realize that churches are not businesses and must not blindly follow business practices. We must be grounded in biblical truth and in scriptural admonition. In every seminar I teach on church revitalization, I call for churches to get back to the preaching of the Word as the foundational element for revitalization. We cannot afford to miss that point or underestimate its importance.

I am convinced, though, that if a business leader would recognize that businesses need not die, we should even more strongly believe that churches need not die. Do businesses die? Of course. Every day, businesses large and small shut their doors. But the point that Adizes makes is that businesses do not have a lifecycle that necessarily leads to death. As human beings, we understand that we die because of the Fall (Gen. 3). When Adam and Eve sinned, death entered the world. Paul reminds us of this fact in Romans 5:

> Therefore, just as sin entered the world through one man, and death through sin, in this way death spread to all people, because all sinned. In fact, sin was in the world before the law, but sin is not charged to a person's account when there is no law. Nevertheless, death reigned from Adam to Moses, even over those who did not sin in the likeness of Adam's transgression. He is a type of the Coming One. (vv. 12–14)

What we have, even outside of the distinction between the human life and the church organization, is the Living Word and the Holy Spirit. Paul continues:

> But the gift is not like the trespass. For if by the one man's trespass the many died, how much more have the grace of God and

the gift which comes through the grace of the one man Jesus Christ overflowed to the many. And the gift is not like the one man's sin, because from one sin came the judgment, resulting in condemnation, but from many trespasses came the gift, resulting in justification. Since by the one man's trespass, death reigned through that one man, how much more will those who receive the overflow of grace and the gift of righteousness reign in life through the one man, Jesus Christ. (vv. 15–17)

We speak of death, but the reality is, believers live forever and experience eternal life. Therefore, the death scenario is altered. In fact, theologically, the whole "death concept" is redefined by what we know about Christ and His death. Everyone lives eternally; it is only those who repent and trust in Christ who experience eternal life in Christ.

Not to digress, but we must understand that a person who dies without Christ, unfortunately, lives forever in eternal separation from God. Jesus was exceptionally clear about this fact in the Gospels. Of the four times that the word *Hades* is used in the Gospels, Jesus is the speaker in every instance. The word *gehenna*, translated most often as *hell*, is found twelve times in the New Testament. Jesus used the word eleven times (the twelfth time is found in James 3:6). This word is perhaps the most graphic of the descriptions used in the Bible for those who are lost without Him. They do not cease to exist; they are lost in torment.

Thus, we are reminded of the mission of the church but also of the eternal nature of the church. We, the church, live forever. Therefore, do not give up on the church, the body of Christ, and do not give up on the local church. Harry Reeder reminds us:

No matter what Satan and his kingdom of darkness bring to bear upon Christ's church, he will never succeed ultimately. For Christ has promised that His church will prevail, not the gates of Hades. The success of this task has been secured in three ways.

The success was secured first at the Atonement. Jesus Christ not only died for sinners, He died for His church. The Word of God clearly states that the Atonement was sufficient and efficient to save sinners. It is also clear that it was sufficient and efficient to make the church of Jesus Christ sanctified, washed, and glorious in triumph.

It was also secured at Pentecost. There she was empowered by the fullness of God with the outpouring of the Holy Spirit, so that the church of Jesus Christ is the one eternal, supernatural, and divine institution chosen as God's instrument to be the body of Christ bringing the Gospel of Christ to bear upon this world. She is not a reservoir of blessing, but an instrument of blessing for the glory of Christ.

Finally, the success of the church has been secured in the promises of God's Word. We are told that the church built by Christ will never be overcome by Satan but will tear down the citadels of darkness, taking captive every thought to make it obedient to Christ.[6]

My point is that we must not lose hope for the church. Do churches die? We read from the prognosticators of the number of churches dying and closing their doors every year. Even Gary McIntosh laments this phenomenon, saying that

congregations tend to traverse a predictable life cycle that is similar to a bell curve. A church is prone to rapid growth in the first fifteen to twenty years of its existence, followed by a leveling off of growth onto a plateau for another twenty to forty years. Then follows a slower decline over the next thirty to forty years until the church either closes its doors (dies) or eases into an unhealthy period of stagnation.[7]

But my premise is that churches do not have to die. Mark Clifton and Sam Parkison echo this sentiment, when they write:

In the whole of the New Testament, no passages describe the life cycle of a church. In fact, in the Scripture only one passage describes the potential death of churches. And do you know how they are in danger of dying? Have they simply "run their course"? Is it that they've simply "run out of steam"? Did they "become disconnected from the community"? "Oh well, these things happen." On the contrary, these churches are in danger of dying because Jesus is threatening to kill them (so to speak). Chapters two and three of Revelation document King Jesus calling seven churches to faithfulness. The judgment which will result from their refusal to repent is that Jesus will "remove [their] lampstand[s]" (Revelation 2:5). Did you catch that? Churches don't die because they unavoidably have an expiration date on them. Churches die because Jesus judges them. When a church fails to submit to the lordship of Jesus, and when a church cares more about their own comfort than sharing the gospel with a lost world, that church will die. And it will be Jesus who brings about its death as a judgment for their disobedience. On the flipside, this means that as long as a church is made up of Christians, revitalization is still an option. Repentance brings life on the individual level.[8]

Why Is Revitalization So Difficult?

It is in the midst of this reality of dying churches that we are called to revitalize. But revitalization is so difficult. The simple reason for this difficulty is that churches wait to try to embrace the changes necessary to get them on a growth plane until they are at a point of desperation or despair. Even then, churches are highly resistant to change. Notice the pattern toward death.

The new pastor arrives and there is a sense of hopefulness until he tries to initiate change or deal with some of the reasons for the church's difficulties. Once a church moves away from the growth plane, it moves toward a nostalgic look to the past and latches onto the power groups or families in the church. They bring a feeling of stability because of their longevity of service and membership. The pastor finds opposition, because, when the church does not sustain the immediate attendance bump that they experienced during his first few months, and now old problems have resurfaced, leaders call into question his leadership skills, the search committee's recommendation for him to be the pastor, and why people continue to leave the church. Therefore, within three years, he has either been fired or has found another place to go.

Mark Clifton offers an excellent evaluation of this time of nostalgia and questioning. If anyone wonders why declining churches struggle to get back into a growth mode, Clifton provides some good answers. He diagnoses the characteristics that define a dying church, offering these eight perspectives:

1. **They value the process of decision more than the outcome of decision.** Dying churches love to discuss, debate, define, and describe. They live for business meetings—even if few people attend them. In the absence of meaningful ministry through the church, they often spend their time meeting together to make oftentimes meaningless decisions. Some of this can be attributed to the fact that they simply don't understand how to reach the community. They can't comprehend how to begin to make real and significant change, but they can still meet and go through the motions of the things they have done for decades.

2. **They value their own preferences over the needs of the unreached.** Dying churches tend to make their preferences paramount. Those preferences can include music, programs, preaching styles, uses of the building, resources shared with those outside the church compared to resources used for those within the church, and a host of other things. The point is this: Most members of the congregation focus on their own desires in these decisions instead of what would meet the needs of people who don't know Jesus.

3. **They have an inability to pass leadership to the next generation.** They may want young people in the congregation. They may complain endlessly about the lack of young people in the church, but they have no strategic plan in place to identify and place into positions of real and meaningful leadership young leaders, or worse yet, they tend to fight any attempt to put young people in charge of significant ministry efforts.

4. **They cease, often gradually, to be part of the fabric of their community.** Members of dying churches rarely live within walking distance of the church. They have typically long ago moved to other parts of town. What was once a community church has become a commuter church. . . . If the church closed tomorrow,

it is likely that no one in the neighborhood would fear losing their quality of life or that the neighborhood would be negatively affected.

5. **They grow dependent upon programs or personalities for growth or stability.** Declining churches reach for programs and personalities they believe will turn the church around without embracing the changes needed to become healthy again. . . . No doubt, as a dying church reflects on its heyday of growth, members recall a particular pastor or two who, by sheer force of personal charisma and leadership, moved the church to a new level. Or they recall a program or series of programs that once attracted all ages of people to become involved in the life of the church.

6. **They tend to blame the community for a lack of response and, in time, grow resentful of the community for not responding as it once did.** Declining churches are often slow to believe the problem lies within. Instead of embracing Jesus' call to transform their nearby community, they tend to believe they need protection from it. They may make attempts at community engagement. They may have a block party or give away food and clothing, but when no one attends Sunday school or morning worship as a result of these attempts, the church's resentments are reinforced. . . . Dying churches often mistakenly assume the community is there for them. They see the community as the resource from which they can grow, when in fact they need to understand that the truth is just the opposite. The community is not there for the church; the church is there for the community.

7. **They anesthetize the pain of death with over-abundance of activity and maintaining less fruitful governance structure.** Church members who remember the church's heyday often feel intense disappointment over the current fruitlessness of the church. Instead of making the necessary changes to turn things around, they simply get busy doing "church stuff." Many believe that to quit these longtime practices of the church is to abandon the legacy of previous generations.

8. **They confuse caring for the building with caring for the church and the community.** Often, declining churches see no

difference between the building and the church. The primary motivation of the remaining members may be to "keep the church doors open" or to make sure they don't lose possession of the place that has meant so much to them throughout the years. . . . To be frank, it is easier to spend time and money fixing a building that doing the hard work to become an indispensable part of the fabric of the community.[9]

It is easy to see how the church eventually moves into the period of polarization. Power groups have formed and are functioning. Debates ensue as conflict escalates and, perhaps, becomes commonplace. The dropout rate of members increases and the congregation is left having to decide whether or not to keep meeting. They now become a part of the statistic of the thirty-five thousand–four thousand churches that die annually. Some would rather die than give up their power seat, not realizing that, if the church ceases to operate, they do not have a seat at the table at all.

But this perspective is not the attitude to which we are called. Rather, we are called to believe that there is hope for churches, and to take up the difficult task of the ReClaimed Church. We will come to the processes of revitalization later, but now, we turn to the task of determining factors for growth or decline.

Determining Factors for Growth or Decline

CHAPTER 7

The Three Primary Phases
of the Church Life Stage

The church revitalization process would be much simpler if churches and pastors would recognize when they are in need of revitalization. Unfortunately, human nature and perhaps human pride keep churches from admitting that they have this particular need. So many churches end up closing their doors, not because they could not revitalize, but because they either denied that they needed it until it was too late or they gave up hope too early.

This section of the book is intended to help pastors and laymen recognize where they are on the revitalization Life Stage. Are they growing, plateaued, or declining? The issue is far greater than numbers. Churches can manipulate numbers, ignore numbers, or even stop gathering data altogether. For example, in the Southern Baptist Convention, an apparatus is provided for every church to gather its statistical data annually and to share it with the convention at large. The importance of the apparatus is that it aids the church in knowing concretely where it stands numerically. The information, while made available throughout the convention, is not intended to be used to embarrass a church or to discipline a church.

Sadly, numerous churches never gather this information, and, therefore, are in the dark as to their own growth or decline. As already addressed, churches will ignore the current state of their congregation and live nostalgic lives, remembering the years gone by. All the while, the church will continue its slide downward until it reaches a bottom from which it cannot climb. Churches and pastors must be willing to evaluate their situation honestly and to realize that help is available. Though it seems hopeless, there is hope for the church in need of revitalization. Al Mohler reminds us:

> Replanting churches requires both courage and leadership skills. A passion for replanting a church must be matched by skills in ministry and a heart for helping a church to regain a vision. Church replanting and church planting are both frontlines of ministry and mission. And I am excited to see what God will do in this age with a generation of young pastors ready to plant and replant gospel churches with unbridled passion.
>
> Of course, this will also require that churches in decline recognize the need for radical change and reorientation in ministry. No young pastor worthy of his call will be excited to assume the pastorate of a church that simply wants to stem the losses or slow the decline by doing slightly better than the congregation at present. Sadly, many of these churches will die by congregational suicide. Unwilling to be replanted, they simply want a slower decline. This is disobedience to Christ.
>
> Given the scale of our need, this rising generation needs to be known as "Generation Replant."[1]

This section is quite simple, yet it will help pastors and church members explore their attitudes, opinions, processes, and actions that give proof to their actual position on the Life Stage. Hopefully, it will help them to make changes in course and direction in order to get the church back onto a growth plane.

A church will find itself in one of the five phases of the Life Stage. These include:

Birth → Growth → Plateau → Decline → Death

The first and last are easily recognizable. The middle three, however, present the greatest challenge. We use the idea that the church is somewhere on the Life Stage, but we must remember that the people are the church. At this point, we have to look beyond the church as an organization or an entity. It is people, along with their attitudes, actions, and behaviors that demonstrate where the church finds itself on its Life Stage. Is it growing, sitting on a plateau, or is it declining?

It is interesting to note how church revitalization is a growing need among all evangelical and even nonevangelical churches, both in the United States and worldwide. It appears that, in the areas where the church has existed for several centuries, those church groups are experiencing severe decline in numbers and attendance. The few exceptions are areas where Christianity is outlawed or persecuted, a fact that opens the door for a whole new discussion about church growth. The Center for the Study of Global Christianity at Gordon-Conwell Seminary reports that the areas of the world where Christianity continues to grow include South Central Asia, Eastern Asia, the Arabian Peninsula, and Western Africa. According to their statistics, nineteen of the twenty top countries experiencing an increase in Christianity are in Asia and Africa.[2] Unfortunately for those of us in the West, North America and Europe do not rank in these statistics.

These reports are somewhat skewed because of how they define Christian and evangelical. Gordon-Conwell admits that

> like other sociologists of religion, the CSGC utilizes a strict methodology of self-identification. That is, if an individual claims to be Christian, then the CSGC considers him/her a Christian. Mormons and Jehovah's Witnesses are classified as "North American Independents" in our typology. This means that they are members of traditions born in the American context as renewal movements within Christianity who self-identify as Christians.[3]

Even the American Religious Identification Survey uses a very broad definition of Christian as opposed to Evangelical Christian when they report that

> Eighty-six percent of American adults identified as Christians in 1990 and 76 percent in 2008. . . . Thirty-four percent of American adults considered themselves "Born Again or Evangelical Christians" in 2008. The U.S. population contin-ues to show signs of becoming less religious, with one out of every five Americans failing to indicate a religious identity in 2008. . . . The "Nones" (no stated religious preference, atheist,

or agnostic) continue to grow, though at a much slower pace than in the 1990s, from 8.2 percent in 1990, to 14.1 percent in 2001, to 15.0 percent in 2008. . . . Based on their stated beliefs rather than their religious identification in 2008, 70 percent of Americans believe in a personal God, roughly 12 percent of Americans are atheist (no God) or agnostic (unknowable or unsure), and another 12 percent are deistic (a higher power but no personal God).[4]

In spite of these discrepancies and poor definitions, the fact that the number of people who identify as Christian has dropped while those who consider themselves a "none" has grown demonstrates the quandary of the American church. The population continues to grow, but the growth of the church is not keeping up with the increases. In fact, all indications are that the church is losing ground.

The Growing Church

The growing church finds its identification in health, vision, and ministry. Mark Dever provides a precise list for defining church health. In fact, his definition of a healthy church is quite interesting, because it focuses on character rather than activity. He writes, "a healthy church is a congregation that increasingly displays the character of God as his character has been revealed in his Word." He then lists his "marks" that are the identifying characteristics that give evidence of a healthy church. These include "expositional preaching, biblical theology, a biblical understanding of the good news, a biblical understanding of conversion, a biblical understanding of evangelism, a biblical understanding of membership, biblical church discipline, biblical discipleship and growth, and biblical church leadership."[6] Tony Morgan adds to these some physical indicators of church health. These include growing over time, being unified, bearing good fruit, multiplying ministry, embracing that which is new and expecting change, and being generous.[7]

Stephen Macchia offers similar characteristics for a healthy church but adds a chapter called "The Process of Becoming a Healthy Church." These three steps include a challenge: to maintain the proper balance, to maintain a season of growth and change, and to pursue requisites for renewal.[8] Macchia seems cognizant that even the healthy, growing church must have an understanding of renewal and revitalization. These decisions are not just for the declining church that decides it needs to revitalize; healthy churches must embrace the changes that will keep them on the growth plane.

Since the growing church is primarily characterized by health, it is possible that some churches can grow but have unhealthy growth. Unhealthy growth comes when a church adds people due to a church split in another congregation, a surge of people through special events that do not lead to discipleship (thus their attraction to the church is only through the big event, not the church or the gospel), when the church grows because of its location but exhibits few of the other qualities of health, or when it grows more because of methods, technology, marketing, or pastoral personality than it does the gospel. I have said countless times to students and in seminars that not all church growth is biblical church growth. Therefore, when I use the term "growing church," I am identifying it as a growing church that embraces the characteristics of health.

When a church is healthy, it then is positioned to experience growth. Its vision drives the church toward ministry, mission, and multiplication. As it develops strategy that allows the church to fulfill its vision, the quality of its ministry increases and the extent of its mission grows. It is a church that has developed a biblical church vision and believes that it is called by God to fulfill that vision.

The Plateaued Church

The plateaued church reaches its plateau because it starts to be characterized more by tradition than by vision. The vision is still apparent, but it no longer is the driving force for the church. Ministry begins to be more directed toward members than having a balance of in-reach and outreach. The quality of ministry, facilities, and activities levels off, where before, the church set a standard of excellence. In fact, instead of being driven by vision, the motivating force becomes its programming. Structure shifts from fulfilling the vision to administrating the programs. Form trumps function. The church becomes more concerned with what it does and keeping those forms than with why it exists. Routine becomes the norm, and the primary purpose of the staff is maintenance and management, as the church moves toward an inward focus.

Tony Morgan addresses that issue and identifies the common symptoms of churches that have moved toward a plateau that he identifies as maintenance and an inward focus:

1. ***Attendance growth plateaus or begins to decline.*** Every church experiences the ups and downs of attendance patterns. One indicator of a church in the maintenance phase, though, is that these plateaus or dips extend from months to years.

2. ***The church becomes insider-focused.*** The voices of the people inside the church become louder than those of people outside the church and outside the faith. When this happens, attendance numbers, group connections, event participation, serving, and other indicators of health may stay strong, but the number of salvations and baptisms starts to decline.

3. ***The vision stales.*** There's still a vision. In fact, it might be painted on the wall in the lobby of the church. The problem is, the vision fades over time. Some churches in this maintenance season have a vision, but it's too generic. . . . In other instances, there's an established vision, but the systems and methods have become more important. The *how* becomes a higher priority than the *why*.

4. ***Ministry silos begin to form.*** Rather than one team pulling in one direction, ministries begin to prioritize their programming over the health of the overall church. . . . Before you know it, the church has become program-driven. There are lots of new programs and new events, but they're pulling people in different directions and creating complexity.

5. ***The church becomes overstaffed.*** On the way up the life cycle, more and more resources became available to hire more people any time a new challenge popped up. Rather than raising up volunteers to engage the ministry, more of the ministry shifted to staff. Compounding this issue is the fact that most of that hiring happened from the inside (people already attending the church). Without fresh perspectives from the outside, staff teams

tend to do the same thing they've always done and hope for different results.

6. *They remain financially healthy.* When a church is experiencing growth and health on the left side of the life cycle, there are more unbelievers and new believers in the church. They typically don't give. That's why growing churches are stretched financially. Mature churches have a higher percentage of Christ followers who have matured in their faith, including their generosity and obedience about giving. That's why it's not uncommon for a church in the maintenance phase to be financially healthier than a church experiencing strategic growth on the opposite side of the cycle.[9]

Morgan provides additional insight into this idea of the church plateau with some common symptoms of an inwardly focused, maintenance-minded church:

- The bulletin is loaded with announcements. Usually this is an indication the church is focused on programs rather than people.
- There are lots of meetings. The more inwardly focused a church gets, the more board and committee meetings there are to talk about buildings and budgets.
- You don't hear and share stories of life change. Instead, you're more likely to hear about all the activities happening in the church.
- There's only one Sunday service. Inwardly focused churches are more concerned about knowing and seeing everyone.
- If there is more than one service, there are multiple styles of worship. There's a traditional service, a blended service and a contemporary service. That's an indication the worship is more about the preferences of people who already attend the church.
- Change of any sort is resisted. It doesn't matter how big or small the change. . . . Inwardly focused churches are more interested in preserving the past.
- People are not inviting their friends. Because of that, the gut reaction may be to teach more on evangelism, but that typically doesn't fix the problem.[10]

What are the root causes, then, of a plateaued church? Morgan addresses the symptoms and evidences. Phil Stephenson provides insight into why churches plateau. He lists these ten reasons:

1. *Missional drift.* Churches can easily drift from the biblical purpose of fulfilling the Great Commission to the institutional purpose of survival.
2. *Change resistant.* Initiating change often results in conflict. Change must take place for a church to move off its plateau, but few leaders want to negotiate the process needed to initiate and implement that change.
3. *Leadership deprived.* A plateaued church needs a leader who is willing to show the way to the next level of effectiveness. A congregation deprived of leadership will quickly move from plateaued to declining.
4. *Overly tolerate.* Churches often tolerate sin, infighting, complacency, and disruptive activity out of a misguided sense of acceptance. The longer the acceptance, the deeper the rift. The deeper the rift, the stronger the hold on the plateau.
5. *Functional dysfunction.* Much like families and individuals can learn to function with dysfunction, so can churches. Their dysfunction becomes their norm. "Many churches never experience a comeback because they want the community to change while they remain the same." [Quote from Ed Stetzer and Mike Dodson in *Comeback Churches* (Nashville: B&H Publishing Group, 2007), 16.]
6. *Systems suffocation.* Every church has systems in place. In many churches, the systems become their reason for existing. This results in *how* the church does things (systems), rather than *why* they church does things (mission).
7. *Cloudy clarity.* Clarity in mission and vision is critical for the continued effectiveness of a church. Over time the clarity of direction can become cloudy, confusing, and downright chaotic. Lack of clarity freezes a congregation, or it wanders off in the wrong direction.

8. *Vision indifference.* A visionless church can be rekindled in its vision, yet a community of faith indifferent in its glimpse of a preferred future is on dangerous ground.
9. *Inward inertia.* "The focus of the church is on itself, on what it needs to succeed." [Quote from Reggie McNeal in *The Present Future* (San Francisco: Jossey Bass, 2003), 25.] This is the corporate attitude of plateaued churches. They are hurting so they focus inward.
10. *Success syndrome.* Churches that have had a season of ministry effectiveness tend to continue to do the same thing over. They bask in their success. They wrongly believe that what got them to where they are will get them to where they want to be. The past success of the church has put blinders on its current state.[11]

Part of the difficulty of a church that moves into the Plateau Stage is that it remains essentially healthy. If they were biblical in their founding, they are most probably biblical now, or at least they will be in their theology and preaching. The primary factors that move a biblical church from growth to plateau will be that the methods become more important than the vision and the church becomes program-driven rather than vision-driven. Functionally, the church is still a biblically based congregation. They still have a biblical understanding of the good news, a biblical understanding of conversion, a biblical understanding of evangelism, a biblical understanding of membership, and a biblical church discipline. They have begun to plateau, however, in the realm of biblical discipleship, growth, and church leadership. Those areas seem to be the first to collapse under the pressure of internalization. At this point, it is not so much about biblical knowledge as it is biblical application.

The dangerous part of the Maintenance Plateau, and why churches need to recognize if they are in this stage of life, is that it gives a false sense of security. The church is still relatively healthy, but the years of growth have brought a weariness upon the congregation. If the church has been fortunate to have the same pastor during this time of birth and growth, he is now over fifty, having come to the church in his late twenties or early thirties. The church is now in its second generation of members, who are far less aware of the mission and vision of the church than the founding generation. People have grown relatively satisfied with their spiritual lives and are drawn now to something more stable than growing.[12]

Decades ago I had a woman and her family leave our church because of the constant pressure to grow, both numerically but also spiritually. She was one of our musicians, and her husband was a Vietnam vet who suffered somewhat from PTSD. They did not leave angry, but in her conversation with me, she said, "Everything in my life is constantly changing. The one thing that I need to stay the same is my church." A static church would bring comfort to her in her world of turmoil. So, they joined a church that was stable and satisfied, and they both became quite happy there.

Gary McIntosh warns, though,

> Being on a plateau is often a comfortable place, with little to threaten the life of the congregation. A plateau is much like hypertension, which is called the silent killer by medical professionals. Hypertension has few, if any, outward symptoms, but its effects over a long period of time are still life-threatening. A church on a long-term plateau faces a similar situation. Plateaus, at least ones that last for three or more years, are life-threatening, silent killers. This is particularly true when the plateau has lasted one or two decades.[13]

Robert Dale echoes this sentiment when he writes:

> Organizations die on autopilot. Coasting and admiring past victories leads to organizational inertia, a plateau. Since the plateau is at the apex, the institutional situation appears secure. But this quiet time in organization life is really a lull before the storm. Soon some stakeholders may become uneasy with simply settling for the past or at the sense of being stuck; they will rock the boat.[14]

Therefore, it is essential that a church recognize its Life Stage and begin to make the necessary adjustments, especially if it ascertains that it is on a plateau and that the congregation has grown satisfied with its position. The church may seem healthy, but decline is near.

The Declining Church

As the church begins its downward spiral, a noticeable change occurs within its ministry and mission. At this point, attendance, finances, membership, and other tangible watermarks are on the decline. As a result, ministry becomes compromised in quality and in expanse. Growing churches are identified through their vision. Plateaued churches are identified through their programs. Declining churches are identified through their structure. In other words, the church becomes more concerned with how it is operated than with the impact of its ministry or the vision it has for the future.

Gary McIntosh offers this insight into the characteristics of a declining church:

1. **The few newcomers that come to a declining church do not know the vision or mission of the church.** Third-generation members seem to have forgotten why their grandparents founded the church. Older members try to restore the former mission and vision of the church to avert decline, but doing so never seems to work as they hope it will.

2. **Newcomers find it extremely difficult to get involved in ministry.** Even though they would like to serve, and older members say they have done their part, it's just too difficult to get involved.

3. **Morale polarizes among different groups in the congregation.** Some groups are discouraged, while others continue to see some hope for the future. Together the church members have little or no sense of their corporate identity.

4. **The church buildings are beginning to show their age, and deferred maintenance is becoming a problem.** There is definitely more space than needed at this time in the church's life cycle.

5. **Everything is well organized and structured, but it is difficult finding people to serve on the numerous boards, ministries, and committees.** The present form of ministry determines its function, and it is nearly impossible to close an existing ministry.

6. **Programs that no longer serve their original purpose are allowed to eat up resources simply because they have always**

been there. As the many programs use up resources, the real needs among members of the congregation are not met.

7. **Few changes are proposed, and no changes are considered that depart from the status quo, which someone jokingly notes means, "the mess we are in."** Clearly it is the ideas of insiders that are preferred over those of any newcomers.

8. **The pastor is self-satisfied with past achievements and focuses primarily on the management of the existing program.** While overseeing a declining staff, the pastor hopes that the church will experience a quick turnaround involving little pain but knows such a thing rarely if ever happens in real life.

9. **Worship attendance is declining.** A few visitors attend worship but rarely return for a second visit. Members no longer feel the worship service is of high enough quality for them to bring family and friends. The worship service is out of touch with the younger generations, and some notice that when high school students graduate, they begin attending a different church in town. Even older members are increasingly absent from worship, with close to 55 percent of formal members coming only two or three times each year.[15]

It is for these reasons that Dale and others describe a decline in the church that moves from nostalgia, to polarization, to questioning, to dropout, to death. If the church finds itself on this side of its Life Stage, it is at critical mass to seek a turnaround. The longer a church stays in a decline and the further down it moves on its Life Stage, the more difficult it will be for the church to go through a targeted revitalization. At some point, the only hope that the church has is to do a Restart or a Legacy Replant, which will be discussed later. Both of these routes are viable and honorable options, but require significant changes from the church's original founding. Churches must recognize whether they are growing, plateaued, or declining, and then make the necessary adjustments as precipitated by their Life Stage. That process is what revitalization is all about—making the changes necessary to get the church back on and keep it on a growth plane.

CHAPTER 8

Distinctive Characteristics
of the Life Stages

O ne of the most helpful exercises for a church is to examine the characteristics that define and distinguish each Life Stage, and then to determine, not just where the church at large is, but also where the leadership is.[1] These characteristics become visible through the decision-making processes of the church and the perspective that the church has regarding growth. These ideas are critical, especially for the church that is on a plateau but does not realize its position in its Life Stage.

One of the greatest hindrances to churches revitalizing is that they do not know that they need to revitalize.[2] Moving to a plateau or into decline is normally a very slow process. The concept presented by George Barna in *The Frog in the Kettle* fits very well here. He uses the idea to illustrate how subtle many changes are that come upon us, so much so that we sometimes do not even notice those changes.[3] That fact is especially true as a church moves from growth to plateau. Growth slows to a trickle. Normally, the church continues to baptize its children and sees some additions as individuals and families join the church. What they fail to realize is that their additions only equal the number of deaths and transfers that the church experiences. The appearance is that the church is growing, but the reality is that the church has plateaued. No one notices the changes. Then as those additions slow down further and the deaths and transfers either increase or even remain stable, the church moves into a barely noticeable decline. It seems that this pattern has always been true for the church, and people's attitudes toward growth have been modified by the slow changes the church has experienced as it has moved from growth to plateau to decline.

It is critical that the church examine its attitudes, not only about growth, but about its present situation. This section will help church members discover how their outlook has changed as the church has changed, becoming more adopting of the church's current situation and more adapting to its Life Stage. Remember, *revitalization is the process by which the church learns to embrace the changes necessary to get it back on and keep it on a growth plane.* Notice the attitude parts of the definition: learns and embraces. People not only need to know how to revitalize their church, they must be willing to embrace the changes that are necessary. This exercise will help them to discover their attitudes about growth and to recognize what changes have to take place in their mind-sets in order to get the church back on a growth plane.

Vision

Growing churches have a vision that looks to the future. For them, vision provides the means to own God's strategic direction for the church. The church embraces who they are and what they aspire to be. In this sense of destination, they focus more on the future than they do the present. It is the dream of the church, and they envision what the future looks like and how they will fulfill their mission.

Plateaued churches have traded the present for the future. In many plateaued churches, they have reached the goals set in an earlier stage of life. Now that they have reached those goals, it is time—in their minds—to enjoy the present. The congregation enjoys stable finances, a full staff, good programs, and adequate facilities. They begin to hold onto the past as they enjoy the present.

Declining churches live in the past. Their initial vision was fulfilled long ago or was never really achieved. They remember the days when the church was strong. The talk of the leadership is about the great days of the church. Their attitude is not one of hope but of nostalgia. They love their current pastor, but their affections are more on a pastor from another era. Vision is rarely, if ever, mentioned. Today is about survival.

Strategy

Growing churches take the dreaming stage and turn it into a doing stage. The vision tells us who we are and are going to be, the mission clarifies the action of our vision, and the strategy offers the specifics of how the church will accomplish these things. For churches that started with a vision, this next step is a natural part of their maturation.

Plateaued churches embrace the status quo. It is the point of satisfaction for where the church is at its present state. While it may still embrace its vision, it loses focus on a strategy that will best enable it to fulfill its mission and reach its vision. This station in life says that the church must begin to take care of itself. Language like "charity begins at home" creeps into conversations.

Declining churches have no plan. The vision is no longer valid or visible; therefore, the church has no plans for growth. Strategy turns more toward survival. The purpose of meetings is to determine how the church can continue to exist, not how it can fulfill its vision. Language includes words like *cut* and *shut down* rather than *build* or *grow*.

Ministry

Growing churches focus on meeting the needs of the community. It is not that the church ignores the needs of the congregation. Meeting congregational needs is done through small groups and leaders trained for this specific purpose. Members welcome ministry and understand that it is a church body concept, not a pastoral staff or leadership expectation. Meeting the needs of the community is primarily done in order to engage the community with the genuineness of the gospel. Ministry has a gospel perspective.

Plateaued churches want to avoid the crises, problems, and difficulties of ministry and focus primarily on ministry for the congregation. This attitude develops in a priority of taking care of those in the status quo rather than in researching and structuring the church to meet genuine needs. Members develop an expectancy that the pastoral staff will do most of the ministry and, therefore, the church begins moving into a state of self-preservation. Meeting needs outside of the church is more of a program that is supported by a few members but not the populace at large. Its primary motive is to allow members to feel good if they help others in need. The goal is far less about reaching those to whom they are ministering at this point.

Declining churches move to do ministry that cares for the control group. Since attendance has dropped and fewer staff are available, people are more concerned about the pastor's pastoral care abilities than they are about his preaching or vision. Criticism erupts when the perceived needs of the core group are not met. Needs are more about opinion and feeling than they are about ministry and the gospel.

Mission

Growing churches develop a clear mission strategy regarding how their churches plan on fulfilling the Great Commission. They understand the mission is as important as ministry. Budgets reflect this mission perspective, with growing amounts of resources going to support mission efforts. Mission is used in language as something that the church does together.

Plateaued churches move mission from a strategy to a program. It begins to involve fewer people in the church and becomes less about what the church does and more about programmatic philosophy. Support for denominational or network missions remains strong, but because mission has moved to a program that the church does instead of the character of who the church is, a growing sentiment develops to move mission to a secondary level behind ministry. Evangelism translates to something that the pastor does.

Declining churches have lost their sense of mission. Mission becomes more about denominational support than about the church fulfilling the Great Commission. The church cannot see itself as a sending congregation, but merely as an organization that exists for support and information. Mission is talked about as an event of the past rather than a present experience. Evangelism is something the pastor is paid to do.

Structure

Growing churches build structure for increased growth as a foundation. The structure is in place to help the church continue to grow. Therefore, the church is committed to developing healthy leaders, and they give the ministry away to these leaders. Members understand that ministry is done by more than just the pastoral staff and are accepting and excited about these opportunities. The control structure of the church moves further away from a single group or person. Leaders understand that they are servants, not dictators. Committees, programs, and ministries exist to further the vision, not the structure itself. Members encourage the evaluation of ministries and the structures that support them and favor their elimination when they become ineffective.

Plateaued churches view structure as a means of maintenance. Committees, ministries, and programs are about preserving the status quo, with those who have the strongest investment in the church serving as control agents. Structure is not about preparing the church for future growth but about being in control of the decisions and direction of the church. The foundation grows smaller, as fewer people are a part of the power group. The structure of committees, programs, and ministries is purposed for the church to care for its own.

Declining churches develop structure for self-preservation. Structure has no vision concept or growth imperative. The church structures itself in order to survive. Those serving take on more roles, so that the structure of the past can be maintained, but accomplishment becomes less apparent. Conflict arises as groups compete for finances and personnel.

Motivation

Growing churches find the motivation for their existence in their vision. The church has determined God's vision for them, and they are driven to allow that vision to determine everything they do. Their vision is big enough to allow them to dream big dreams for God. Everything they do flows out of that vision.

Plateaued churches find the motivation for their existence in their programs. Since the programs have developed out of their vision and are a part of the strategy and structure, they have made the mistake of substituting program for vision. Programs have existed long enough that the church is identified more by its programs than anything else. Everything they do flows out of these programs.

Declining churches find the motivation for their existence in their structure. Vision is lost and strategy is ineffective, but structure gives them stability. The church is identified now by its committees, buildings, and organization. Control and power are primary elements of this structure-oriented church. Programming is stale but the structure keeps everything alive. Everything they do flows out of this structure.

Emphasis

Growing churches emphasize reaching the community with the gospel. Since a gospel-centered vision drives the congregation, they see the world as their mission field. The community is not a resource from which they are to draw but the reason for which they exist. Growing churches are led by Scripture that gives command and calling to love people as themselves and to make them into disciples.

Plateaued churches emphasize ministering to the congregation with programs and staffing. A part of the programming is evangelism, but outreach takes a back seat to inreach. Since they have reached a time of stability and can look back on days of strong evangelism and outreach, it is time to care for the flock. Little notice is given to a decline in baptisms or conversions. The church is satisfied and presumably healthy.

Declining churches emphasize caring for the remaining members through acquiescence. Since power struggles have highlighted the movement of the church from plateau to decline, the church at large fears a greater splinter of the membership. Therefore, instead of leading the church to a deeper discipleship and an understanding of membership, the church accepts poor behavior, power moves, and negative voices. Finances are critical; therefore, no one wants to confront the disgruntled or the power group. Members know that unhappy members will not leave quietly and will take others with them; therefore, the populace remains silent and offers little resistance to the power brokers.

Faith

Growing churches exhibit a high-risk faith. While trusting God would be a quality that all churches believe they have, growing churches, in determining God's vision for their church, pursue it with little or no hesitation. They expect God to guide, provide, and protect them and are willing to risk all for the sake of the vision.

Plateaued churches demonstrate a careful faith. They are committed to the success of the church, but they view faith as protecting what they have in resources and what they have accomplished. Launching new ministries is acceptable as long as it occurs in a safe environment. Oftentimes leadership will prioritize following sound business practices rather than biblical principle, all for the sake of managing risk.

Declining churches move from a careful faith to a protected faith. They determine that they must protect their limited remaining resources, as these things become increasingly endangered. They interpret faith as holding onto what they have with the hope that God will bring about something better for them in the future. Finances, ministry, and mission are all interpreted in light of human effort rather than divine provision.

Decisions

Growing churches make faith decisions. Although they consider the physical evidences of finances, resources, and personnel, they move forward with the high-risk faith that has been a part of their DNA. Decision-making is drawn more from how it helps the church accomplish its vision more than it is on resources available or the risk involved, since they believe that God is the source of their vision. Details do not have to be complete in order for the church to move forward.

Plateaued churches make analyzed decisions. While trust is a factor, leadership evaluates the need for the decision with the resources available in financing and personnel. The belief is that, if God wants them to move forward with this decision, He will first demonstrate how He will provide for it. The church undertakes new ideas only when the provision is available or foreseen.

Declining churches make fearful decisions. While a lack of decision is commonplace, when a decision has to be made, it is made fearfully, knowing that another poor decision can lead the church into greater decline. Their protected faith leads them to believe that caution is the best alternative to risk. Decisions are made for how they best help the church in its present decline, and whether they can keep the church from falling into any more immediate decline. The church does not consider the long-term effects of a decision. The combination of self-preservation, protection, and introversion means that the church does not step out in faith. They carefully preserve what they have.

Service

Growing churches seek to involve people through gifting. Part of the church's discipleship has been to help members discover their service passions and spiritual gifts. These passions and gifts are connected with needed areas of service. Due to the young age of the church, less emphasis is given to length of membership and more toward spiritual gifting.

Plateaued churches involve people in service through position. Since the church has expanded its structure to include committees, programs, and ministries, some of which are needed and some of which exist by default and history, a committee on committees and a nominating committee seek to fill these slots, first through the people that they know, and then by availability. Choices for important committees are made because of a person's duration of membership and areas of influence. Little thought is given toward gifting or ability. Movement is made to protect certain decision-making committees, thus beginning the decline into control and power and for protecting the status quo. Less important committees are filled with newer people.

Declining churches fill positions by availability. The church has not fully adjusted their structure to match their decline, and there are usually more spots available than there are people to serve. Oftentimes, term limits are overlooked or suspended so that important positions can be filled and maintained. Control of important positions becomes paramount as the church has moved into a protection mode.

Stewardship

Growing churches give through a perspective of generosity. Need is a greater motivator than obligation. Since the church is made of many new Christians and younger people, giving is not as consistent as in older congregations. Therefore, more time is given to the why of giving than just to the responsibility. This generosity characterizes all areas of stewardship, including giving, service, and involvement. Budgets are planned based upon mission.

Plateaued churches practice stewardship through responsibility. These churches now have older members who have learned the biblical responsibility of giving and stewardship. Therefore, they give systematically and faithfully. The church is most probably at its pinnacle in financial stability. Budgets are planned based upon projection rather than on need or mission.

Declining churches give out of survival. Members give sacrificially because they know that the church cannot remain open without their gifts. The mission of the church is the subsistence of the church; therefore, members give with a sense of purpose. Giving oftentimes becomes burdensome because the need increases as the membership dwindles.

Leadership

Growing churches plan for future growth by embracing fresh leadership. Leadership is not so much about position or power but about service and growth. The church recognizes that new ministries will be created in the future, so current leaders invest in new Christians to become future leaders. An attitude even exists that part of their responsibility is to send out leaders to be on mission in other churches and parts of the world.

Plateaued churches lead through entrenched leadership. The church has existed long enough to see leaders rise to take positions of importance in the church, and those positions are strongly protected. Established positions are filled by trusted members, while new members are given opportunities to prove themselves through lesser, decision-light committees or ministries. An avenue still exists for newer people to serve, since structure has been fully developed. The church, though, demonstrates care in who serves in which positions.

Declining churches are led by surviving leadership. Since new leadership is not available, most leaders have filled those positions for a number of years. Deacons have served for decades, as have those in the discipleship ministry or the children's ministry. People serve out of necessity more than calling. No investment is made in training new people because of the oxymoronic perspective of protectionism and the threat of the new.

Growth

Growing churches grow through profession of faith. Priority is given toward evangelism and ministry to the community, resulting in conversions to Christ and baptisms. Gospel presentations are common, and multiple entry points are offered for people to trust Christ and become part of the church. Members are equipped and encouraged to share their faith, and the church provides numerous opportunities for members to be involved in outreach. A primary portion of the budget goes toward evangelism.

Plateaued churches maintain through transfer of letter. Baptisms continue but move more toward the baptism of members' children rather than outside conversions. The age of baptismal candidates becomes younger, while the transfers by letter match those who letter out of the church. The plateau occurs because the church is no longer reaching the unchurched and the unsaved. Evangelism is programmed and takes on a lesser priority than does ministry to the church. Entry points into the church become more controlled, and evangelism receives a lesser portion of the budget, both in percentage and in actual numbers, than in previous years.

Declining churches decrease through negative growth. Those leaving outnumber those who join. Transfers by letter are rare, and baptisms are even more uncommon. For declining churches that practice immersion, the baptistry has often found a substitute purpose, such as for storage. The church experiences the conflict of failing resources and therefore the inability to reach out to the community or to minister to its own members. As a result, the church continues to lose people and move from decline into death. Little to no money is designated for evangelism. More money is set aside for flowers for the dead than for winning the lost.

The So-What?

In examining these characteristics, every leader and, hopefully, every church member can discover where their attitude is regarding growth and revitalization. Doing revitalization is difficult because, as so many leaders say, no one wants to admit that they need revitalization: a revamping of their discipleship, yes; a revewal of their commitment, yes; a redevelopment of their strategy, yes; but a need to revitalize? No. Admitting that need is problematic and even traumatizing for some. Though it may be difficult, it is necessary for the sake of Christ's church. So utilize this apparatus, as it can be helpful in awakening the church to its Life Stage and to the positive need for revitalization.

Life-Stage Chart

	GROWING	PLATEAUED	DECLINING
VISION	FUTURE	PRESENT	PAST
STRATEGY	DOING STAGE	STATUS QUO	NO PLAN
MINISTRY	TO THE COMMUNITY	FOR THE CONGREGATION	FOR CONTROL GROUP
MISSION	GREAT COMMISSION	PROGRAM	NO MISSION
STRUCTURE	FOUNDATION	MAINTENANCE	SELF-PRESERVATION
MOTIVATION	VISION	PROGRAMS	STRUCTURE
EMPHASIS	REACHING COMMUNITY	CONGREGATION	REMAINING MEMBERS
FAITH	HIGH-RISK FAITH	CAREFUL FAITH	PROTECTED FAITH
DECISIONS	FAITH DECISIONS	ANALYZED DECISIONS	FEARFUL DECISIONS
SERVICE	THROUGH GIFTING	THROUGH POSITION	BY AVAILABILITY
STEWARDSHIP	GENEROSITY	RESPONSIBILITY	SURVIVAL
LEADERSHIP	FRESH	ENTRENCHED	SURVIVING
GROWTH	PROFESSION OF FAITH	TRANSFER OF LETTER	NEGATIVE GROWTH

Steps toward Revitalization

CHAPTER 9

Determine a Revitalization Strategy

I n order to lead a church to become a ReClaimed Church, the church and the pastor need to understand what processes and opportunities are available. Church revitalization can be done in a variety of ways, depending on the circumstances, resources, and Life Stage of the church. Regardless of the situation, the pastor must have a strategy tailor-made for his church's context.

Revitalization Types and Processes

Essentially, three types of revitalization exist from which a church and its leaders can choose. Each one has its positives and negatives and requires some hard questions to be asked in order to determine which of the types would work best in the church's current situation.

Restart

A church restart (also called a replant by other revitalization leaders) is where a church decides that it cannot continue to exist in its current state. Therefore, it chooses to restart as a congregation. The qualifications listed address the reasons why the church needs a totally new relaunch of itself.

The Requirements

1. New Name. Churches on the decline will often find that multiple reasons exist for why the church is in its present state. These include:

- The community has changed but the church has not changed with it.
- The church has developed a bad reputation in the community because it has traditionally fired its pastors, used the community for its own growth (for example, the sign out front that reads "Come Grow with Us," which the community interprets as "Come Help Us Pay Off Our New Building"), the church's ministries were far more internal than external, the church has viewed itself in a different socioeconomic status than the community.
- The church has a reputation of being dead, lethargic, uninviting, or unfriendly.
- The church has lost the reason for its existence.

Great care must be taken at this point. If at all possible, the church name needs to be ReClaimed. Just putting up a new sign will not change anything in the community. The people around the church know better. In fact, a part of being a ReClaimed Church may be ReClaiming the name. On the other hand, designing a new name strategically allows the church to create a new community image and to project an entirely new mission outlook. The name should be drawn from the development of a new vision, mission, strategy, and structure for the church and should reflect that vision. Do not rush into finding a new name.

In the past, churches drew their names from the street on which they were located, the nearest river or creek, or a popular biblical name (not to say that Calvary Church is a bad name!). In today's culture, church names that reflect the congregation's vision and mission best communicate to the community the purpose and connection that the church has with people. Creating a new name is a strategic part of the church restart.

2. New Pastor. I want to take great care in communicating this qualification. What I don't mean is that if every struggling church got rid of its pastor, the church would grow. Many churches have fired the last five pastors, yet still have not grown and now have a bad reputation in the community. Obviously, the best time for a church to decide to do a restart is when they are either pastorless or have a pastor who is nearing retirement. Pastors in churches that need to restart need to ask if they are equipped, willing, and ready to lead the church in that direction. A new pastor may mean a physically new pastor or it may mean a pastor who makes the changes to his mind-set, ministry, and mission to essentially recreate himself into a revitalization pastor. This process can be quite effective, especially if he and his congregation enter into a new covenant relationship with each other.

Sadly, there are times that the pastor needs to leave in order for the church to get back on the growth plane. He carries with him too much baggage, too much pain, and too much rejection to be able to effectively lead the church to revitalize. It is an incredibly difficult decision, and one that the pastor should generally be allowed to make on his own, utilizing the counsel of wise men around him. While it is true that many pastors have too short of a tenure, it is also true that pastors can stay too long.

John Maxwell, in his book *The 21 Irrefutable Laws of Leadership*, teaches that, when a leader starts a new leadership position, he comes with a certain amount of "change" in his pocket. When he makes good decisions, that change increases. When he makes bad decisions or difficult ones, he loses change. And as Maxwell says, "When you're out of change, you're out as the leader."[1] The way a pastor knows he's out of change is when people no longer trust him or follow him. It does not necessarily mean he lacks character or is untrustworthy. Those facts could be true. It simply means that, in that particular situation or church, his decisions or lack of decisions have led his people to lose trust in his leadership. In leaving the church, he may find that the next place of service fits his skill set and gifting. It will allow him and his family to heal, and it can become an effective transition, especially if he approaches the new ministry opportunity with the perspective of having learned from his mistakes and having made necessary spiritual, personal, and emotional changes in his life.

Again, I want to take great care in addressing this issue. I am like Opie on one episode of *The Andy Griffith Show*. A friend was taken to the woodshed to be spanked. When Andy asked Opie if he thought his friend deserved it, Opie replied, "I don't want to say. After all, he is one of my own kind."[2] I love pastors, and I will always be a defender of the pastor. After all, they are one of my own kind! I also love the church, and I realize that sometimes change is a good thing. Personally, in ministry, I think that I have stayed at a church out of the stubbornness not to allow a group to run me off. In hindsight, I needed to be more sensitive to the leadership of the Holy Spirit and not listen to those who play in the devil's workshop. While Satan sometimes uses God's own people to do his bidding in attacking a pastor and causing him to get distracted and discouraged, pastors need to stay focused on God's plan for them. This fact is especially true in leading a church through revitalization.

A new pastor, called with the perspective of a restart in mind, can genuinely be a catalyst for leading the church to revitalize. When this qualification is possible, the church must take great care in calling their new pastor, evaluating his gifting and skill sets not just on the value of good preaching, but with the standard that he is called and driven toward revitalization. Churches must not make the mistakes of becoming impatient or panicking. During this time of transition, they have the opportunity to find God's man for their church. Once he arrives, they must remember to treat him as God's man.

3. New Leadership. While it is true that sometimes the pastor shares in the fault for the decline of the church, it is equally true that church leaders bear that guilt. Throughout a church's history, power struggles can probably be traced, whether at the birth of the church that happened through a church split, or at some point on the church's Life Stage whereby family members, matriarchs/patriarchs, age groups, or the status quo decided it was time to take control. These power struggles have caused the church to lose focus and to lose members.

Therefore, the best scenario is for all leadership to step down for a season. The deacons need to resign, the Sunday school teachers need to give up their positions, and the committees need to dissolve. The process for restarting will help explain how the church will survive during this interim period. At this moment, though, leaders need to stop leading and take time to heal and rejuvenate spiritually. They are tired, hurt, and perhaps angry. The burden of carrying the church debt, the church history, and the church reputation has been overwhelming. The season of not leading allows them to refocus on their own spiritual journey, their commitment to the church, and their part in the decline and revitalization of the church. Since leadership is a critical part of the success and ReClaim of a church, those currently in positions of leadership need time for personal revitalization. Stepping aside for a season allows for this restart.

The Process

1. The church restart signs a covenant agreement. Once the church determines that a restart provides its best course of action, it needs to follow a specific process that will get it back on a growth plane. One critical part of this process is for the church to covenant with another church and with a church network, convention, or denomination that teaches, promotes, and supports church revitalization through a specific contract of agreement for how the process will take place. The reason is because, once the church starts to experience some level of turnaround, the leadership will be tempted to ignore the remaining parts of the process and the requirements and will jump back into the very habits, structures, and attitudes that brought them to the point of decline in the first place. This step cannot be emphasized any stronger.

A church with which I was consulting had agreed to do a replant. They were down to just a few people and had reached the point of desperation whereby they were probably going to have to close their doors because of the lack of finances. The mistake I made was in having only a verbal agreement with the church. (I was not charging for my services as a consultant due to their dire financial needs.) We began the process of the restart, and everything was moving along very well. Without a contract of some kind, though, I had no way of ensuring they would keep their part of the agreement. I met on several occasions with the church leadership to spell out specifically what was required for a restart. They verbally agreed to everything. Once things started to turn around, they immediately jumped ahead of the process. In their defense, it was purely out of excitement, not rebellion. Their attendance grew significantly, but then one of the old leaders rose up just as he had in previous years. Many of their problems—especially the bad name that they had in town—were due to poor decision-making and a general attitude of hatefulness. These things now surfaced again. Fortunately, deeper scars were avoided and the church is back on track, but that entire crisis could have been avoided had I had them agree to a specific, physical covenant of revitalization.

Obviously, a covenant agreement is not the solution to every problem. A church could choose, at some point, just to ignore the covenant
altogether, but in a spiritual agreement between brothers and sisters in
Christ, biblical integrity would lead all parties to honor the agreement.
Having it in writing assists in reminding everyone of the commitments
and promises made by all parties involved. A sample covenant agreement
is included in the appendices.

2. The church shuts down for a specified time. The point of this
step is to let the church reinvent itself, so to speak. These months of shutdown allow the church to heal, to refocus, and to reconsider who they are.
If the pastor believes, along with the church, that he is ready to tackle this
assignment, it gives time for him and the church to learn, research, and
grow together in the revitalization process. It would even be advisable to
remove the church sign, if possible, during this period of time. Anything
that identifies the church must essentially cease. The church has not
closed its doors; it is just preparing for its grand reopening.[3]

3. The church works to rebuild vision, strategy, and structure.
The details of this process are outlined in the fourth section of the book,
so I will not take time to visit those ideas here. The rebuild will include
both the visioning aspect of the church and the structural portion,
including the church's constitution and by-laws. Oftentimes these docu-
ments need updating but also revising so that the church restart can lay a
positive foundation that enables it to get back on a growth plane. A poor
foundation of rule and polity can prevent the church from having a successful restart, regardless of its vision or strategy.

Part of the reason for the church temporarily shutting down, though,
is so that it can focus on re-vision rather than on programs, committees,
budgets, and ministries. Without a designated time of shutdown, the
church will continue to do what it has always done and continue to get
the same results. To shut down essentially means that, instead of empha-
sizing corporate worship that is open to the public, it focuses on personal
worship and waiting on God. We see this idea when Jesus prepared the
disciples for the birth of the church. Luke records:

> While he was with them, he commanded them not to leave
> Jerusalem, but to wait for the Father's promise. "Which," he said,

"you have heard me speak about; for John baptized with water, but you will be baptized with the Holy Spirit in a few days."

So when they had come together, they asked him, "Lord, are you restoring the kingdom to Israel at this time?"

He said to them, "It is not for you to know times or periods that the Father has set by his own authority. But you will receive power when the Holy Spirit has come on you, and you will be my witnesses in Jerusalem, in all Judea and Samaria, and to the end of the earth." (Acts 1:4–7)

Note that Jesus commanded them to stay, pray, and wait. God would move at His pace. Kenneth Gangel comments, "What a lesson for us . . . wait. Don't rush off into ministry unprepared. Don't carry on the Lord's work in the strength of the flesh. The only way we can fulfill Christ's command to witness is to be under control of the Holy Spirit who energizes us for service."[4] Gangel provides the simple explanation for why a church needs to wait. They need to connect with God's Spirit in order to make the changes and decisions necessary for a restart.

4. The church meets with core groups and seeks to grow through small groups. The church, at this point, does not give up on evangelism or outreach. While they must focus on re-visioning, they can also grow through small groups. It may be one small group that meets in someone's home. It could be a couple of groups that meet in the church building or at a coffee shop, but then meet together as one to focus on the re-vision.

Remember that one of the primary purposes of moving away from corporate church to small groups is to eliminate the clutter of church so that the church can refocus on its future. If all the small groups do is have a Bible study, then they have failed in their ultimate purpose. Together, they need to work on personal growth, developing community, and preparing themselves for change and the future. Corporately, they need to be involved in creating a new vision, a new strategy, a new mission, and a new structure for the church. Even if the church has a small group for children and for students, these groups can be and should be included in the process. After all, they will become leaders in the church in the future. Additionally, if the church wants to reach younger families and people, it had better incorporate them into leadership now. Otherwise, they will leave with all the others.

5. The church partners with a healthy church that can provide leadership, counseling, and workers. This step helps answer a common and important question: *Where will workers or leaders come from if all current leadership resigns?* It is important for the church to partner with a healthy church that is willing to take the church replant on as a part of their own mission strategy. Healthy churches plant healthy churches. Healthy churches replant healthy churches. Therefore, it is paramount that healthy churches discover the need and the benefit of coming alongside a declining church and being a partner in church revitalization. Healthy churches are essential in church revitalization.

During the time that the declining church shuts down, the sponsoring church sends people to lead Bible studies, to help the church develop its new vision and focus, and to demonstrate what a healthy church and healthy relationships look like. The sponsoring church also makes itself available to provide counsel and wisdom as the church prepares to relaunch. They serve to encourage the declining church and to fill the necessary voids that occur when the church shuts down. Additionally, if the pastor has decided to stay, he must meet regularly with the healthy church pastor to be mentored, encouraged, and challenged. It may be during this shut down that a new pastor emerges, either from the healthy church or through the church's denomination or affiliations. The healthy church must be directly involved in leading this process, not as a demagogue of control, but for the sake of wisdom and balance. This process needs to be spelled out in the covenant agreement. If the church has made poor decisions in pastoral selections in the past, they need guidance for choosing the right man of God for their church. The healthy church leadership can provide this guidance, and it is part of the reason why the declining church establishes this type of covenant agreement.

6. The church sets a launch date for the announcement of the new name and for reestablishing corporate worship. The best date for a relaunch is Easter Sunday. The worst dates for a relaunch are other holidays, the summer months, or time-change Sunday in the spring. A fall launch is possible if the church develops something really creative for this time of year, even on time-change Sunday. During the months that the church has shut down, it has developed a new name, a new vision, a new strategy, and a new structure. The sponsoring, healthy church encourages its missionaries to be present for the church relaunch, but they move away from leadership over the next several months as agreed through the covenant. Some of them may choose to stay with the relaunch. This decision must be agreed upon by the leaders of both congregations, as Satan can get a foothold by creating jealousy, suspicion, and hurt feelings. The situation then becomes unhealthy for all groups involved. The purpose of the healthy church sponsorship is to get the declining church back on track so that it can have a healthy relaunch. The process demands great patience, an incredible willingness to change, and a deep commitment to ReClaiming declining churches. As much as churches need to become healthy churches to plant healthy churches, they also need to be healthy churches that *replant* healthy churches. The mission is one in the same.

> As much as churches need to become healthy churches to plant healthy churches, they also need to be healthy churches that *replant* healthy churches.

Legacy Replant

In some situations, a congregation is unable to make the transition into a new congregation. Factors such as the advanced age of the congregants, significant demographic changes in the community, or just an unwillingness to make the changes necessary to survive require that a different plan of action be created so that this church continues its legacy. Mark Clifton cautions about doing a replant just for the sake of holding onto a building. He warns, "Don't try to replant a church that no longer has a neighborhood around it. In a replanting situation, your surrounding neighborhood is your primary mission field. If the church exists to serve the local community but you no longer have a local community, you may have no reason for a church. Move somewhere else."[5]

A church, however, that has a viable piece of property can become an incredible help to a church plant that can focus on the surrounding community. While securing a building should not be or become the primary focus of a church plant, a building in a targeted community can provide not just a meeting place, but space for expansion, ministry, and discipleship. The reason many church plants are limited in the scope of their ministry is not because of a lack of vision but because of the inability to provide necessary space. A legacy replant can help solve that dilemma.

Unlike the church restart, a legacy replant does not require the legacy church to make any major changes as to how they worship. The process for this replant is as follows:

a. The legacy church, the new church plant, and any sponsoring churches, conventions, denominations, or networks sign a covenant agreement. The covenant agreement will cover the process for the legacy replant. All parties must be in agreement with the covenant and must adhere to its requirements. If not, the chance of success will be greatly diminished. Part of the discussion has to be denominational affiliations. If the legacy church is an active member of a particular denomination, they will be hesitant to enter into this type of agreement, fearing that the church plant will not honor that same commitment. Right or wrong, one of the nuances of this type of agreement is that both parties must take into consideration the other's feelings, commitments, theology, style, and purpose. The easiest partnership occurs between two churches who share a denominational or network connection. When that connection is not present, the partnership becomes more difficult. It is for that reason that the two churches enter into a covenant agreement that addresses these issues.

b. The legacy church continues to meet and worship as always, keeping its pastor, if possible, and its style of worship. Agreements will have to be made as to where and when the two congregations meet, but the legacy church is encouraged to continue doing what it always done.

c. The legacy church partners with a church plant that utilizes and shares facilities, costs, and people. One of the reasons that the legacy church would be near to closing its doors is because of the inability to take care of their building. By sharing costs, the legacy church's financial burden is lessened and subsequently will be able to invest their money into other ministries. The church plant benefits because it has access to a usable building to which it would not have access outside of this partnership. If developed carefully, it provides a winning relationship for both churches.

d. Both churches cooperate by helping the other church function. The benefit of this type of agreement is, not only that the legacy church continues to worship and serve God in ways that are familiar to them, but it also allows for both congregations to understand multiple generations and styles of worship, and to provide for the needs of one another. For example, the legacy church could serve as preschool or children's volunteers during the church plant's primary worship gathering. The church plant could find ways to fill leadership or service roles for the legacy church. As the church plant seeks to develop new ministries, the older adults of the legacy church certainly could provide a portion of that ministry venue. There is also a possibility that, as the church plant attracts younger families, it may also connect with older adults who would feel more comfortable with the legacy church. While the church plant must not get distracted from its vision and strategy, it certainly should keep in mind the ways that it could help the legacy church in outreach.

e. The legacy church eventually deeds the property to the church plant. As the legacy church continues to age and sees the end of their ministry in that building, either through the death of members or through an advanced age that prevents their attendance, they need to begin the process of legally deeding the property to the church plant. Several issues must be considered.

1) State laws need to be referenced since every state may have its own particular nuances regarding the transfer of property. It would be a tragedy if the process was put on hold or canceled due to the improper filing of papers or the missing of a legal requirement. The legacy church must also know the rules that govern them through their denomination. In some denominations, churches are completely autonomous. In others, autonomy is limited through the hierarchy of the denomination. Those issues must be addressed and researched so as not to hinder the transfer of assets.

2) If the two congregations are members of the same denomination, this transfer of property becomes simpler. Depending on the denomination or association of churches, the property could be deeded first to the association of churches. Then the association of churches transfers the property to the church plant. The benefit of this process is that it helps the church plant develop deeper roots with the denomination or association by working directly with them in the deeding of the property.

3) If the two churches do not share a denominational connection, it probably means that the legacy church needs to deed the property directly to the church plant. As one who now works for a denomination, I know that it may cause problems or resentful feelings within the denomination if the property is transferred to a non-member church. While Christians should be above this seeming pettiness, Satan drives wedges between churches, not only through theology, but through hurt feelings, jealousy, and suspicion. The legacy church model obviously demands that both churches are growing spiritually as they tackle this method of revitalization. Communication, discipleship, and spiritual depth are essential qualities to ensure a successful legacy replant.

f. The church plant utilizes the legacy church name in some fashion in order to keep the legacy alive. This method is called a legacy replant for a reason. The legacy church wants their work to continue long after they are gone. While every church must be extremely cautious about memorials (i.e., putting names on pews or other parts of the church or naming buildings after church members) the church plant can use wisdom in honoring the ministry of the legacy church while not limiting their ability to use or change the building.

The legacy replant is a genuine possibility, especially for older congregations or ones that have lost their connection with the community. A church plant within their building can redirect the church to begin to reach the once neglected neighborhood and get the gospel to those who are outside of Christ. If 3,500–4,000 churches are closing their doors annually, this method merely substitutes one church for another, but it still stems the tide of church demise. The legacy of the church lives on.

Targeted Revitalization

This type of revitalization entails the entire church vision, structure, and strategy. It is a targeted decision by a congregation to go through the process of revitalization. It is, in all actuality, this type of revitalization that should be ongoing in every church.

I asked a colleague of mine, J. D. Payne, who served on the faculty of The Southern Baptist Theological Seminary and now serves as the pastor of church multiplication for the Church at Brook Hills in Birmingham, Alabama, a question several years ago regarding when a church plant will encounter issues that will require definite change. In my opinion, Payne is one of the premier mission strategists for evangelicals, so I value his opinion greatly. I recently asked him for an update on his thoughts and observations. He said that many times in church planting, the church sets a vision of what they want to accomplish within their first three to five years. For example, the church wants to plant another church by its third year. When that time arrives, other matters often lead them to believe they are not ready or other things take priority, preventing them from accomplishing their original vision.[6]

For example, I worked with a church plant that is now about ten years old. The church had grown to an attendance of 250 but now was down to about fifty members. They were very much style driven, adopting a certain method of worship and ministry taught through a church planting network. Unfortunately, other churches had relocated to their area that utilized this same methodology, and the church plant was not able to compete in worship or in ministry. As some members left, other issues surfaced that caused a greater exodus of people, eventually resulting in a mere shell of the church it formerly was.

When I began working with them, I worked with the leadership, walking through these various styles and ministries, evaluating them based upon their effectiveness. When I met with the congregation at large, I shared with them the changes that needed to happen in order for the church to rebound and revitalize. One couple responded, "But we like how we do worship." My answer to them was, "That style is hindering your growth and is actually causing your church to decline." Their response to me was very disturbing but so apropos. They said, "We do not care if it is causing us to decline, we do not want to change what we do."

The good news is that the church did survive. When I began working with them, after the fallout, about thirty-five people remained. By the time of their relaunch, they were averaging 150 and were totally self-supporting. This situation demonstrates how most all churches will be in need of some type of revitalization. Pastors of established churches and of church plants need to learn the art of the Targeted Revitalization. It is an ongoing process for every congregation, calling for the church to refocus and to re-vision.

A good question to ask at this point is: When does a church need to consider going through a targeted revitalization? Here are some ideas.

1. When a ministry loses its effectiveness. For example, cold-contact evangelism used to be effective in most parts of the United States. In today's culture, fewer areas exist that are open to having a stranger come to the door unannounced. In fact, in some areas, this type of evangelism does more harm than good. Churches that have always used this method of evangelism, and only this method, probably have seen significant results in the past but now are finding their numbers dwindling. The church has not lost its evangelistic zeal. It simply needs to change, and in a way that probably will not come easily. The same thing is true of giving a public invitation; in some situations, the public invitation has lost its effectiveness. (As one who has for decades given an invitation after preaching and has written on the biblical foundation for a public invitation, I find this statement a difficult one to make.) It does not mean that the church does not invite people to salvation; it just means that they are finding new ways to accomplish this task. The change will be incredibly difficult to accept in some churches, but if the invitation has become ineffective, then it needs to be revitalized. A targeted revitalization is in order so that the church can make the changes necessary to remain effective in reaching those outside of Christ through the preaching of the Word.

2. When church members lose interest in a ministry. Churches minister in many capacities, but when the pastor and his family are the only ones who show up to conduct a particular ministry, it is time to reconsider. The change is far more than just stopping the ministry. There may be a theological or spiritual reason for the lack of participation, or it may require a logistical shift. The ministry needs to be revitalized or revamped.

3. When conflict becomes commonplace. When churches become focused on problems or create the proverbial "mountain out of a molehill," the church is in need of revitalization and revival. The revitalization may be more in a spiritual area than a technical one, but when a church begins to fight amongst itself, it means that it has lost its vision and purpose.

4. When Great Commission evangelism becomes secondary. In most church plants, evangelism is a strong priority. Ministries, outreaches, and strategies all have an evangelistic purpose and focus. As a church settles in, it can reach a point of complacency that is deadly. Members are satisfied because they see people being baptized, never realizing that they are comfortable because the only baptismal candidates are their children. Now that the church has grown, outreach has become far more internal than about reaching the community, and genuine evangelism has become secondary. In fact, a resistance to evangelizing those who are outside of the church may be present (although few will openly admit it).

5. When the church's original vision is lost or not followed. Vision changes, as does strategy. The original vision that the church had could possibly be fulfilled, if the vision was somewhat limited. It also could be outdated in the sense that the community or the city has changed. The vision from fifteen years ago was adequate, but now it is outdated or stale. It is time for the church to re-vision and restrategize. Revitalization is necessary because people are still connected to the vision; they do not follow it but will resist changing it.

6. When a church needs to make changes to grow spiritually. Churches start with particular styles, ministries, or structure because they have limitations to resources, people, or finances. As the church grows, so must its structure for discipleship and worship. People, however, become satisfied with these programs or processes. They like the songs sung or the type of material studied, even though both are lacking in spiritual depth. The church originally sang simpler songs because that is the style that allowed their musicians to lead in excellence. A more surface discipleship material was utilized because most of the discipleship leaders were young Christians themselves. Now, as the church has grown and matured, it is time to move to a deeper level of worship and discipleship. The change is not something that can happen overnight, therefore, the church must strategically work through a process of targeted revitalization in order to grow to the next spiritual level.

7. When the church has gotten into a rut. Similar to the comfort zone, every church faces the spiritual/ministry rut. Doing the same thing the same way every week makes ministry appear easy and familiar. It is difficult to come up with something new every week, whether in preaching, worshiping, or discipling. Anybody can come up with that one creative sermon that wows the masses, but try that accomplishment weekly—even with a worship or preaching team—and it is easy to see how the church can get into a rut. One church with which I consulted was a church plant under a decade old but was certainly in a worship rut. They had a worship team that met on Sunday afternoon and would encourage the pastor to develop a sermon based upon a movie clip that someone on the worship team has researched. Every week, the movie clip would be shown and the pastor would preach a sermon around the movie clip, interjecting Scripture as appropriate. Not only were there some theological issues at play in this method, but the church was in a rut spiritually and evangelistically. The church had stopped growing, but no one seemed to notice. The sermon was more about a clip than about Scripture, and that fact led the church into a spiritual lull. It needed a targeted revitalization that met with resistance but was absolutely necessary to move the church into a spiritual climb instead of a spiritual drought.

8. When the church is ready to go to the next level. At its birth, a church is limited in what it is able to do in ministry and in mission. Its focus is much more restricted and concise. Its primary purpose is to grow and survive. As the church moves through the obstacles to growth and solidifies its existence, it becomes time to move to new ministry and mission. If the church does not make these changes, it will stagnate and stop growing numerically and spiritually. Thus, the church must look to create new ministry endeavors and choose to engage new mission opportunities. It is time for the church to go to the next level spiritually and structurally, but those changes require strategy. They may not be fully accepted because they demand that some ministries cease while others are birthed. The changes necessitate a reallocation of finances, with more money going toward these new ministry and mission endeavors. Because even these changes are difficult and strategic, a targeted revitalization is in order. Remember that revitalization is the process to help the church learn to embrace change.

Sponsoring Church

Regardless of which revitalization strategy a church uses, it should partner with a healthy church that can provide support for the revitalization effort. Some of that support may come in the form of financial help, but this type of backing should be the least of the kind of assistance provided by the sponsoring church. While a church in decline may fall into financial difficulties, money should not be a motivating factor. If it is, the declining church may fall into the trap of a welfare mentality, and by doing so, set themselves up for failure. When the money runs out, so does the church.

If the declining church follows the pattern of a Restart, a Legacy Replant, or a Targeted Revitalization, the required adjustments will provide additional finances through the elimination of unnecessary programs, the changes in structure, or the addition of a church plant in their facilities. A healthy church that might not be overwhelmingly blessed with additional finances should not refuse an opportunity to help ReClaim a declining church just because of money. Though very visible, money is most probably the least of their problems.

The primary purpose of the sponsoring church is threefold:

1. *To give the declining church an example of and insight into the characteristics of a healthy church.* The declining church needs to see that church health is possible.

2. *To provide leadership personnel for the declining church.* Since it is essential that the leadership of the declining church step away from their positions for a season, the sponsoring church sends members who can help fill the essential positions for helping the turnaround of the declining church. Many leadership positions will be put on hold until the declining church is ready for a relaunch. The focus of the shutdown is to help the declining church make the changes necessary to get back on a growth plane. The leadership from the healthy church also provides the example of how church leaders should lead.

3. *To provide coaching and mentoring support for the members of the declining church.* Since church decline is often traced to a spiritual issue, it is critical that the members of the declining church, along with the declining church pastor, enter into a general coaching relationship or a more specific mentoring relationship with members of the sponsoring church. If nothing changes spiritually for the declining church, the chance for a successful ReClaim is, not just greatly diminished, but most probably guaranteed. Therefore, an essential part of the revitalization process

is spiritual revitalization. The relationships that the sponsoring church brings to the declining church are indispensable for this ReClaim to occur.

Mission Connections

An important part of helping a declining church embrace change and develop the attitudes necessary for growth is assisting the declining church in getting onto the mission field. Declining churches are habitually internalized and focused only on their needs and problems. The fact that they have not had a missional perspective about how to do church is a dominant reason for why they are in decline. The church has become internalized, and that inward view has crippled them.

> The revitalization pastor and his church should find connections to be engaged on the mission field locally, nationally, and internationally.

Therefore, one of the opportunities that the sponsoring church provides for the declining church is mission connections. The revitalization pastor and his church should find connections to be engaged on the mission field locally, nationally, and internationally.

It is also possible for the sponsoring church to help the revitalization church develop other partnerships with healthy churches who desire to have a mission connection with that church going through revitalization. These connections can hasten the revitalization process and remove some of the pressure that the sponsoring church experiences in serving the revitalization church.

Support

It is essential that the declining church and pastor have the necessary support that will help them rebound and revitalize. This support comes in two areas:

1. *Project support.* Through the sponsoring church and mission connections, the revitalization church should have available to them personnel support for major evangelism and church growth projects they undertake.[7]

2. *Financial support.* While finances should improve through the adjustments made in revitalization, it is proper for the sponsoring church to provide limited and perhaps targeted financial help to the revitalization church. This help should be clearly defined in the covenant agreement and must not become a source of welfare for the revitalization church. It is also possible that the sponsoring church could help the revitalization church discover other temporary and focused financial help through their denomination, network, or mission connections.

While obviously extensive, the details of the revitalization plan demonstrate that becoming a ReClaimed Church is no small undertaking. In some cases, it would be much easier to plant a new church than to save an old one. God, however, did not call us to always choose the easy route.

Consider Paul's first missionary journey with Barnabas and John Mark in Acts 13–14. Many of the areas through which they traveled were dangerous. Barely after the journey got started, John Mark left them and returned to Jerusalem (Acts 13:13). In Iconium, they received word that the Jews were planning to stone them, so they fled to Lystra and Derbe. While in Lystra, unbelieving Jews stirred up the crowd, and the resulting mob stoned Paul and dragged him out of the city (Acts 14:8–20). It was a church planting movement, and Paul and Barnabas backtracked through Asia Minor to strengthen the young churches that had been started (Acts 14:21–23). While they accomplished a great work, it was, nonetheless, an extremely difficult work. Sometimes God's work is that way, both in church planting and in church revitalization. When a church is salvaged, though, the difficulty is well worth the trouble.

Conclusion

While there is no perfect scenario for revitalization, it is critical that the revitalization church and pastor develop a specific plan that will lead them from decline to being ReClaimed. The focus of the stages of growth and of decline was to give insight into the current stage upon which a church finds itself and then to make the right decisions, choices, and corrections that will allow the church to embrace the changes necessary to get it back onto a growth plane. Church revitalization is possible for any church, regardless of its size, history, or stage in life. Harry Reeder encourages us with these words:

> So not only does the ministry of church revitalization reflect the heart of God and of Paul, but when it is carried out according to the Word of God, it is also a practical and effective way to meet the current needs of the body of Christ in our land. And I believe this type of ministry could become a catalyst for the large-scale revival that we desperately need in America.[8]

CHAPTER 10

Pastoring a
ReClaimed Church

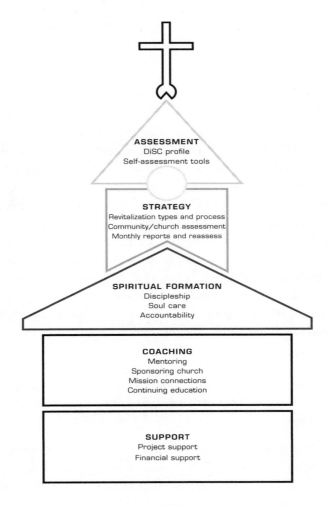

ASSESSMENT
DiSC profile
Self-assessment tools

STRATEGY
Revitalization types and process
Community/church assessment
Monthly reports and reassess

SPIRITUAL FORMATION
Discipleship
Soul care
Accountability

COACHING
Mentoring
Sponsoring church
Mission connections
Continuing education

SUPPORT
Project support
Financial support

One of the reasons church planting has become more effective in recent years is not only because systems have been put in place to help planters with much more than just finances, but because church planting agencies and boards have recognized that not everyone is called or gifted to be a church planter. Thus, they have been more intentional and thorough in the process of commissioning new church planters.

That fact also holds true for those hoping to ReClaim a church. If a pastor is accepting a church that is already in decline, what would be required of him and how can he be successful? How can he assist in revitalizing such a church? There are certain characteristics, training, and assessments that need to occur in order to ensure success.

Personal Assessment

The first step to being successful as a ReClaimed Church pastor is to go through proper personal, spiritual, leadership, and emotional assessments that will help the revitalizer understand strengths, weaknesses, and potential pitfalls. A number of personality profiles and assessment tools exist that help a person make these determinations. One of the most prominent and helpful is the DiSC profile. It is effective in helping determine a person's ability to work with others. It is intended to move beyond just a personality profile assessment. It must be remembered, though, that it is primarily a secular assessment, not a spiritual one. DiSC has recently created a Biblical Profile DiSC Personality System that is intended for use with Christian audiences. It utilizes biblical examples and spiritual gifts for each personality type and then offers an action plan for using these biblical insights in improving relationships.[1]

Self-Assessment Tools

In addition to the leadership profile, a potential revitalization pastor must go through a time of spiritual assessment. Questions should be asked regarding the following for both the husband and his wife.

1. Do both husband and wife share a clear and compelling sense of God's calling to work in revitalization? Is that calling supported and established by fruitfulness in areas of ministry and the confirmation of other people in the church?

2. Do the husband and wife work together as a team? Do they have a healthy marriage and do they manage their family well?

3. Does the pastor demonstrate a godly character and integrity in his personal, public, and home life? Does he fulfill the qualifications found in 1 Timothy 3:1–7?

4. Does the pastor have the right gift-mix to minister effectively within the church and community context? Is he in agreement with the doctrinal distinctives and mission of his denomination or sending agency?

5. Is the pastor a visionary and does he possess a compelling vision for the church? Is he able to articulate this vision and does he possess the drive to see it come to fruition regardless of the cost?

6. Does the pastor possess recruiting skills and a risk-taking mindset for starting new ministries? Is he an entrepreneur?

7. Can the pastor effectively communicate God's Word in a relevant and compelling way through his preaching, teaching, and counseling?

8. Does the pastor actively share his faith with those outside of Christ, especially with those who have no church connection?

9. Does the pastor desire to disciple others, both individually and as a group, in order to develop mature Christians and to build up the body of Christ?

10. Does the pastor utilize skills for helping others discover and use their spiritual gifts?

11. Does the pastor lead as a servant, desiring to identify, recruit, and build a team of people who complement his gift-mix and leadership style and who will follow his vision for ministry?

12. Can the pastor work with a diverse group of people and unite them toward a common purpose and vision?

13. Does the pastor possess a knowledge of church revitalization, church health, and church growth? Can he implement that knowledge into practice?

14. Is the pastor flexible and fluid, able to adjust to the challenges of a rapidly changing culture? Can he adapt to difficult situations and have the fortitude, accountability, and support to continue to move forward?

Another way to evaluate this step and to determine if a pastor is ready for the task and challenge of church revitalization is to ask these nine questions:

1. Will I pray daily for my church and my leadership? Many leaders get so busy doing the work, they fail to take time to pray for God's strength and wisdom to do the work.
2. Will I see this opportunity as a mission field? Both the church and the community are mission fields. We need to approach these opportunities much like an international missionary in his or her new culture.
3. Will I make a commitment for the long haul? Some of the fruit of change often does not manifest until after the leader has been on the field for five years or more.
4. Will I love my critics? Genuine leaders of churches in need of revitalization will have their critics. Will you respond with the love of Christ? Will you pray for your critics?
5. Will I be persistent? Because progress is not always noticeable on a day-by-day basis, it is easy to get discouraged. Stay with it. Stay the course. Be faithful.
6. Will I be an incarnational example in my community? Will I be present and involved in the community where the church is located? Will I demonstrate Christ in deed and words in my community? Will I be an example for the church members to follow?
7. Will I be a lifelong student of church revitalization? New information is coming forth about church revitalization every month.
8. Will I be content? The apostle Paul learned to be content in all situations, including shipwrecks and prisons. Will you be content in the Lord to move forward with church revitalization?
9. Will I be a positive example and encourager for my family? If you are taking a family with you on this journey, they will need your support and encouragement too. Will you be there for them?[2]

Finally, do an assessment regarding these ten simple characteristics of a church replanter. These include:

1. A love of biblical preaching

2. A prayer warrior
3. A visionary shepherd
4. A high tolerance for pain
5. A love for the local church and an affinity for its history
6. A resourceful generalist (be multi-faceted in abilities to lead church ministry)
7. An aptitude for serving in multi-generational contexts
8. Have tactical patience
9. High emotional awareness of your own emotions
10. Spousal support and clarity of call[3]

Spiritual Formation

An important provision made by the sponsoring church and pastor is the continual spiritual formation of the revitalization pastor and his family. This formation should reflect several aspects of growth.

Discipleship/Soul Care

Because of the critical nature and spiritual warfare involved in revitalizing a declining church, it is essential that the revitalization pastor has access to personal discipleship and counseling for both himself and his family. The constant drain on the revitalization pastor's spiritual growth can become a hindrance and even a roadblock to the ReClaimed Church process. Therefore, the sponsoring pastor and church must provide ways for him to grow in his own relationship with Christ and to have opportunities for he and his family to find counsel and help as they battle through some of the difficult situations of revitalization. These opportunities should include ongoing training, fellowship, and specific visits and engagements by the sponsoring pastor and church.

Accountability

Through the monthly reports and individual meetings, the revitalization pastor will be given ongoing opportunities to be challenged, encouraged, and sharpened through an accountability to mentors and spiritual partners. This accountability is not intended as an aggressive form of punishment but as a loving encouragement and balanced discipline. The revitalizing pastor will find great help from these resources as he discovers those areas that require greater work and as he receives reinforcement for his strengths.[4]

Coaching

Closely connected to the idea of accountability is coaching. Some writers make a significant distinction between coaching and mentoring, but here in the context of church revitalization, I see coaching as the big picture, and mentoring as a part of the coaching process. The Brefi Group defines coaching as "helping another person to improve awareness, to set and achieve goals in order to improve a particular behavioral performance. . . . The goal is to improve an individual's performance at work."[5] Because a pastor's personal growth as a Christian is so closely connected to his success as a pastor, coaching and mentoring are more interconnected in the church world than necessarily in the business world.

Regardless of how one might define or distinguish the two concepts, in order for the revitalization pastor to be successful, he needs to have that other person in his life who can help him achieve the goal of pastoring a ReClaimed Church. Usually, the sponsoring church pastor should serve as his coach. That responsibility is nonnegotiable. The sponsoring church pastor must develop structured and regularly scheduled meetings that focus on specific areas of performance and accountability, while also allowing for an engagement with the particular problems or issues the ReClaimed Church pastor faces as he leads his church through change. It is also possible that he will work with the ReClaimed Church pastor as his mentor, though it is conceivable that the ReClaimed Church pastor has the sponsoring pastor as his coach and has another trusted pastor as his mentor. Nevertheless, the coaching process is an essential part of the success of a ReClaimed Church.

Mentoring

Mentoring is a part of the coaching process, though, as mentioned above, it can be separated or can be done by a different person than the revitalization coach. Aubrey Malphurs and Gordon Penfold define a mentor as "one who promotes the development of life and ministry skills for a protégé, primarily by imparting wisdom and skill from lessons learned from the mentor's own life and ministry experience."[6] In this context, they write, "The majority of pastors cannot lead on their own. Most are managers, not leaders. They struggle to pull the leadership trigger. . . . Re-envisioning pastoral ministry is about leadership, not management. Most pastors struggle to lead and need help. Coaches and mentors can help fill this leadership vacuum."[7]

John Maxwell defines leadership as "influence—nothing more, nothing less."[8] He proposes that there are five levels of leadership through which a person can journey and grow. The purpose of the coach and the mentor is to help the revitalization pastor develop his leadership skills and the character necessary to get him to the point of being an effective leader. Maxwell defines the five levels of leadership as:

1. LEVEL 1—POSITION

The lowest level of leadership—the entry level, if you will—is Position. It's the only level that requires no ability or effort to achieve. After all, anyone can be appointed to a position! While nothing is wrong with having a leadership position, everything is wrong with relying only on that position to get people to follow. That's because it only works if you have leverage (such as job security or a paycheck) over your followers. At Level 1, people only follow if they believe that they have to.

2. LEVEL 2—PERMISSION

Level 2 is based on relationship. At this level, people choose to follow because they want to. In other words, they give the leader Permission to lead them. To grow at this level, leaders work on getting to know their people and connecting with them. You can't lead without people, which means you need to learn to like people if you want to lead well!

3. LEVEL 3—PRODUCTION

The best leaders know how to motivate their people to GTD— get things done! And getting things done is what Level 3 is all about. On this level, leaders who produce results build their influence and credibility. People still follow because they want to, but they do it because of more than the relationship. People follow Level 3 leaders because of their track record. The Production level is where leaders can become change agents. Work gets done, morale improves, profits go up, turnover goes down, and goals are achieved. The more you produce, the more you're able to tackle tough problems and face thorny issues. Leading and influencing others becomes fun, because when everyone is moving forward together, the team rises to another level of effectiveness.

4. LEVEL 4—PEOPLE DEVELOPMENT

Level 4 can be summed up in one word: reproduction. Your goal at this level is to identify and develop as many leaders as you can by investing in them and helping them grow. The reason is simple: When there are more leaders, more of the organization's mission can be accomplished. The people you choose to develop may show great potential for leadership, or they may be diamonds in the rough, but the main idea is the same: When you invest in them, you can reproduce yourself. The more you raise up new leaders, the more you will change the lives of all members of the team. As a result, people will follow you because of what you've done for them personally. And as an added bonus, some of those mentoring relationships are likely to last a lifetime.

5. LEVEL 5—PINNACLE

The highest level of leadership is also the most challenging to attain. It requires longevity as well as intentionality. You simply can't reach Level 5 unless you are willing to invest your life into the lives of others for the long haul. But if you stick with it, if you continually focus on both growing yourself at every level, and developing leaders who are willing and able to develop other leaders, you may find yourself at the Pinnacle. The commitment to becoming a Pinnacle leader is sizeable, but so are the payoffs. Level 5 leaders develop Level 5 organizations. They create opportunities other leaders don't. They create a legacy in what they do. People follow them because of who they are and what they represent. In other words, their leadership gains a positive reputation.

As a result, Level 5 leaders often transcend their position, their organization, and sometimes their industry.[9]

The goal of the mentoring relationship is for the revitalization pastor's character to be so spiritually developed that he can influence and lead his church to become a ReClaimed Church. As the British Field Marshal Bernard Montgomery said, "Leadership is the capacity and will to rally men and women to a common purpose and the character which inspires confidence."[10]

Continuing Education

The revitalization pastor—regardless of the form of revitalization he uses to ReClaim his church—should be involved in a continuing education. These events should include participating in seminars, training events, and even formal classes that will assist him in better developing his pastoral and revitalization skills.

The intention of this continuing education is for his personal growth and edification, but it should also be used to target areas of need in the declining church. The revitalization pastor wants to develop skills that will equip his church as they move to that point of turnaround.

Conclusion

Healthy churches need healthy pastors. If a revitalizing church does not make provisions for the pastor and his family to get or remain healthy, the revitalization process will be extremely difficult, if not impossible. Therefore, ensure that the replanter or revitalizing pastor your church takes on has been assessed using various tools. When the pastor is in place, do everything necessary to provide for the spiritual formation of him and his family, and for his continuing education. Though this may seem to slow down the process, it will be much healthier for him, his family, and the church in the long run.

> Healthy churches need healthy pastors.

CHAPTER 11

Reacquire Buy-In

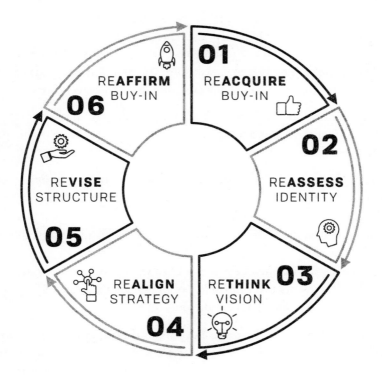

Bill Day, associate director of the Leavell Center for Evangelism and Church Health, conducted research recently to determine the connection of church health with church growth, studying specifically churches in the Southern Baptist Convention. In previous studies, a healthy, growing church was evaluated solely on an increase in church membership over a five-year period. Day's study also examined churches over a five-year period but utilized a new metric for health. He determined that a healthy, growing church is one that demonstrates the following:

1. Total worship attendance growth of 10 percent over five years
2. At least one baptism for the first and last years of the study
3. A worship attendance-to-baptism ratio of 15:1 or less in the final year of the study
4. At least 25 percent of growth must be conversion growth for the final year of the study (He reluctantly removed this requirement due to the fact that some of the conventions who collected this information no longer asked for "other additions," thus removing the ability to calculate conversion growth percentages.)

According to Day, previous attempts at determining church health were inadequate. He provided these explanations for the changes and the more detailed requirements:

1. Many people who are on church membership rolls never attend.
2. A person can be on the church membership roll of a church in Miami, FL but live in Portland, OR.
3. A person can be on a church membership roll and be physically dead!
4. Represents member's presence in the church's community
5. Represents real probability of presence in a church
6. Responds to change more quickly

Day believes that these standards, requiring an evaluation of worship attendance and baptisms, better reflect a proper evaluation of church health and will assist churches and leaders in determining whether or not their church is a healthy, growing church. His conclusion regarding his research, spanning thirty-two years and using membership change as the standard, is as follows:

	Growing	Plateaued	Declining
1978–83	30.5	51.9	17.6
2010–15	24.1	44.2	31.7
Change	- 6.4	- 7.7	+ 14.1

If the metric is corrected to reflect a worship attendance model, the percentage report dramatically changes. Day concludes that, using the worship attendance definition, only 5.4 percent of churches grew between 2010–15, not 24.1 percent. His point is clear: 94.6 percent of churches in the Southern Baptist Convention are in need of some form of revitalization.[1]

Buy-In

This last section gives insight into how any church can revitalize, and the steps that are necessary for that process to occur. While it is true that most churches have fewer than two hundred members, it is not necessarily true that smaller churches cannot revitalize. The smaller the church, the more difficult the revitalization may be, but that fact does not mean that small churches are destined to die. It simply means that the church must begin with a determination that revitalization is no longer just an option for them. It is an absolute necessity.

The process begins with buy-in. Note that buy-in is the beginning point for revitalization, and buy-in is the ending point. The reason is because it does not matter how well a church's leadership plans for revitalization, if the church is not on board and ready to learn to embrace the changes necessary to get them and keep them on a growth plane, all of the work will be in vain. Revitalization allows a church to start anew. Since most churches grow the fastest during their first years of existence, revitalization allows the established church to renew itself and start over. Growth can return to the church.

Process

Buy-in is critical because, most probably during the days of plateau or decline, the church has lost its confidence in the pastoral ministry, in its leadership, in its community, and in the congregation itself. If the church at large is not in favor of embracing even the concepts of change and revitalization, little reason, outside of obedience to God, exists to continue the effort. If buy-in occurs, the church is ready for a new chapter in its

Life Stage. John Kotter and Dan Cohen, in addressing the need for buy-in and moving people and organizations toward change, wrote:

> Our main finding, put simply, is that the central issue is never strategy, structure, culture, or systems. All those elements, and others, are important. But the core of the matter is always about changing the behavior of people, and behavior change happens in highly successful situations mostly by speaking to people's feelings. This is true even in organizations that are very focused on analysis and quantitative measurement, even among people who think of themselves as smart in an M.B.A. sense. In highly successful change efforts, people find ways to help others see the problems or solutions in ways that influence emotions, not just thought. Feelings then alter behavior sufficiently to overcome all the many barriers to sensible large-scale change. Conversely, in less successful cases, this seeing-feeling-changing pattern is found less often, if at all.[2]

Thus, buy-in is critical. People will resist change if it is just presented as a need or as the static process of change for the sake of change. Therefore, address change and gain buy-in by speaking both to the head and the heart of people.

1. Talk with people. In dealing with emotions, talk to the people involved in the change, caring for them as with a family member. Avoid speeches and have real dialogue with church members and leaders. Think through the following guidelines for healthy conversation:

- Quantity—give enough information but do not inundate people
- Quality—be genuine and do not embellish
- Relation—be relevant and communicate how the change will affect people personally and what will be expected of them
- Manner—be clear, brief, and logical; avoid being vague, ambiguous, and wordy

2. Address the emotions in the room. Work to understand how church members and leaders feel about change. Emotions are often triggered by a lack of information, new expectations, a lack of structure or certainty, feeling threatened, and being comfortable with the status quo and not wanting to change. Create acceptance, commitment, hope, and trust by letting people deal with emotions, not just facts. For example, people know that the church is declining. Those are the facts. The emotion, however, is a sense of guilt or a fear of the unknown and the future.

3. Communicate, repeat, communicate, repeat. The leaders who create the need for change fail to understand the frequency of communication that is necessary for people to understand it emotionally and intellectually. As people deal with their emotions, they are less receptive to believing what they hear. Consistency and repetition are key.

4. Vary the medium of communication. When people hear the same message from multiple directions, it has a better chance of being heard and remembered, on both an intellectual and emotional level. Therefore, evaluate what mediums of communication are available for the church and utilize every means possible, including worship services, called meetings, informal conversations, FAQ sheets, the church's website, Bible study groups, committee meetings, and other forms of oral and written communication.

5. Use metaphors, analogies, examples, and stories. Find stories and testimonies of churches that have successfully revitalized. Try to share these stories live or by video. Allow people to engage those who have gone through the process. Make sure the stories are authentic and speak to people's hearts.

6. Develop a succinct presentation about the need for change and what it involves. Besides all the usual methods and forums for communicating the change, it is also useful to have a succinct presentation available for different circumstances. In the presentation, express the following key points:

- Here's what our change initiative is about . . .
- It's important to do because . . .
- Here's what success will look like, especially for you . . .
- Here's what we need from you . . .

7. Be credible. Credibility as the leader is crucial in getting people to buy-in on the change. If credibility is suspect, work to rebuild it before initiating the change. If credibility is low, people will not believe the

message. One of the most powerful ways to communicate a new direction is through personal behavior. Make sure that actions match words.[3]

Tony Morgan makes this important observation about buy-in: "If
a church . . . acknowledges that the end is near, then sometimes they're
willing to do something dramatic to turn things around. It will indeed
take something dramatic. The reality is that churches on life support
need to somehow find their way back to a new beginning. They need to
start over."[4]

That idea is the concept of buy-in. Churches must understand the
urgency of the need and embrace the emotion of what the future holds for
them. In doing so, change is on the horizon, and the future of the church
can be bright again. It all begins with buy-in.

CHAPTER 12

Reassess Identity

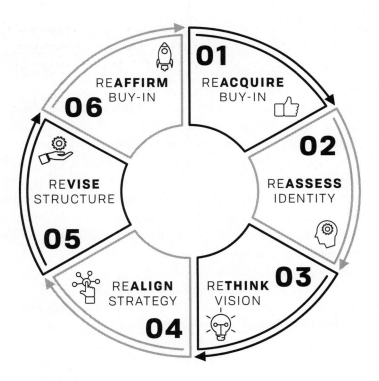

C hurches in need of revitalization usually have an identity problem. With the change in culture, the neighborhood, the age of the congregation, and their Life Stage position, churches struggle with who they are. In order to revitalize, congregations must answer three questions regarding their existence and their identity.

Who Does the Community Say We Are?

In some form or fashion, the plateaued or declining church has stopped reaching the community. Numerous external reasons contribute to the problem. The community in which they are located has experienced an actual decline in population. There are churches that were birthed in a thriving community that now find themselves surrounded more by businesses and manufacturing plants than they do houses. In most cases, the community and the church have gone in different directions. The community has changed ethnically, while the church has maintained its ethnic distinctives. These changes also relate to differences in socioeconomic status, ethics and morals, and the cultural climate. These variations are difficult to overcome.

Additionally, because the church has most probably been in the community for a significant number of years and members of the community have been members of the church or are friends with members of the church, the community knows the inner workings, problems, and sins of the church. If the church has a reputation of dismissing its pastors, if the pastors bear rumors of moral or ethical failure, or if the church is known for power struggles and an unwelcoming atmosphere, one can be certain that the community knows that information. The church believes they are well-respected in the community, while the neighborhood thinks the church is no longer valid, genuine, or friendly.

These and other scenarios demand that the church asks and answers the question: Who does the community say we are? One of the churches that I mentioned earlier that needed to undertake a Legacy Replant was in need for two reasons: 1) the church did not reflect the changes that had taken place in the community, and 2) the church had a bad reputation in the community. Interesting enough, the church knew both problems yet still struggled with the idea of change. In the back of their minds, they could come up with another solution besides change.

Part of buy-in is that the church must be willing to examine the community's attitude toward the church and follow recommendations for repairing or fixing the problems. If the church is unaware of the neighborhood's perspective or if they have simply ignored the evidence, it is important to take them through the exercise of facing the reality of who the community says that they are. There are several ways that this need can be accomplished:

1. Use an outside source to survey the neighborhood. Get help from members of another church or from a mission team to go door-to-door and ask a series of simple and short questions that can ascertain people's opinions about the church. Questions should be open-ended enough to allow people to give more than just a "yes" or "no" answer, and they should be intentionally developed to lead to a question regarding people's opinions about the church and why they would not consider attending that church. The questionnaire must be anonymous and those taking the survey must receive assurance of such.

2. If church members are friends with people in the community, have them ask their friends for their honest opinion. This method is risky and could cause hurt feelings, but church members should be interested to know why their friends do not attend and what needs to change to make the church welcoming again. These questions could also be asked of former members who left the church for another church in town. Again, care must be taken in asking the questions, with assurances given for anonymity, and that the information is going to be used to help the church change.

3. Questions could be asked by local businesses, such as a nearby gas station, grocery store, or strip mall. This type of survey is best done on a Sunday morning by someone not a member of the church who can ask for directions and for that person's opinion of the church. The point of the survey is not to be intrusive or rude but to ascertain public opinion. If the church is not reaching the community, its members need to know what the community thinks of them and why they are unresponsive to the church.

Who Does the Church Think They Are?

This question will provide a great deal of information, revealing some of the obstacles that the church faces. Knowledge of these stumbling blocks provides necessary data as the church prepares itself for change. The purpose of this question, as well as the other two, is to help the church step into a reality that will allow it to embrace the changes necessary to get on and stay on a growth plane.

Oftentimes, the church has an uninformed understanding of who it is. Biblically, the church knows that it is part of the body of Christ. The church is the bride of Christ, the friend of Christ, and the creation of Christ. Practically, many churches in need of revitalization view themselves in a far different light than their reality. The question is not just for the church itself, but it also raises the question about the world in which the church finds itself. Corporately, the church has missed how it has changed and has missed the changes around them that polarized them from the neighborhood and from culture.

> Oftentimes, the church has an uninformed understanding of who it is.

Carey Nieuwhof lists ten changes that have occurred that have caused churches to be out of touch with reality and with culture. These include:

1. **Church Attendance Is Now a Fringe Activity.** With the exception of a few U.S. communities (deep in the Bible Belt), nobody asks which church you attend anymore, because the assumption is you don't go to church.

2. **"All Welcome" Means Nothing.** Almost every dying church has an "All Welcome" sign nobody takes seriously. Think about it, if you didn't go to church, would you take that as an invitation? Next time you drive by a church building, ask yourself, "What would it take to convince me that I can walk in uninvited and participate in what they're doing?"

3. **Regular Church Attendance Is Irregular.** The assumption used to be that if you were a committed Christian, you would go to church every week. In fact, even most growing churches still silently run on that assumption, even as the leaders admit that weekly church attendance is far from the norm. Culture has changed so radically in the last decade or two that even committed Christians aren't in church as regularly as they used to be.

4. **A Band, Lights, and Haze Are Traditional.** You might have cashed in a lot of chips to redo your church's approach to music over the last decade or two. And that's wonderful. But increasingly, having a band and even lights and haze is pretty normal in many churches. In fact, as Tony Morgan first noted a number

of years ago, the way we do worship music in the "contemporary" church is not that contemporary. In fact, the band, guitar, keyboard and lights is the new traditional "rock" worship. The culture has moved on to other music: hip hop, R&B, DJ, pop, and so much more.

5. **The Show No Longer Captivates.** If you're over thirty, you remember the church of your childhood was probably trying to be "contemporary"; they just weren't very good at it. Church often provided a fairly low level of excellence in terms of singing, production, and sometimes, speaking. That has changed massively. With the connection that's happened online, many preachers and musicians have become so much better at their craft. Production levels have soared at local churches. And it's not enough. I mean it's good that we're doing things well. But reaching people is about more than just doing what you do with excellence. It used to be that great preaching and great music grew a church. Now it's more like the cost of doing business. Bad preaching and bad music can kill a church, but great preaching and great music don't automatically generate church growth. Something more fundamental is shifting. And it's not all bad. In fact, it could be the rebirth of the church based on God's movement and activity.

6. **Your Church Members Follow a Dozen Ministry Leaders Who Are Not You.** Go back to forty years ago. Chances are the only pastor a church member knew was the pastor at their local church or their neighborhood church or someone they heard on TV or radio. Even in the 90s and early 2000s, as culture changed, to "follow" another preacher meant ordering their cassettes or CDs or tracking them in a very limited way in the early days of the Internet. Contrast that to today, when many Christians actively listen to, read, and follow more than a few other ministry leaders, subscribing to their podcasts, reading their blogs, and otherwise tracking with their church.

7. **God Has Become Generic.** As the Barna Group's research has shown, even though most Americans self-identify as Christian, almost 50 percent function as post-Christian in their practices

and beliefs. In other words, what people define as Christian and what constitutes genuine Christianity may be two different things.

8. **People Don't Know What They're Converting To.** It's so easy to make assumptions that people who attend your church know what they're stepping into. After all, don't most people know what it means to be a Christian? Well, no they don't. Church leaders will have to become far more innovative in the language and metaphors we use to help people understand the basics of the Christian faith.

9. **Background Understanding Is Often Zero.** In the same way that people don't understand what becoming a Christian means or why it matters, post-Christian people have very little Christian background from which to draw.

10. **No Church Can Be Better Than Some Church.** Our culture has gone through a few decades of people leaving the church. Often there are stories of heartbreak and disappointment there that really sting. But we're moving in real time away from a generation of people who are done with church to a generation that doesn't know church at all. They don't have any hang-ups to overcome.[1]

Churches will often describe themselves as friendly, welcoming, or evangelistic when none of those characteristics are true, and they may never have really been true. Like most people going through difficult stages of life, sometimes those stages are painful, and the easiest way to deal with them is to ignore them.

Who Is the Church Really?

If the church can get to this question, it is on the path to a new start. When a church understands what the community thinks of it and when the church realistically deals with the false image that it has projected, not only to itself but to the world, those painful exercises will lead the church to grow again.

The church must recognize and acknowledge its sin, its shortcomings, its failures, and its successes and the possible resulting pride. It must honor the past and learn from the things it has accomplished. It must also gain knowledge from its failures. Churches will probably be resistant to the demands of a restart or a legacy replant until they see the reality of who they are. It can be an incredibly painful and discouraging experience, so leaders need to be careful in guiding the church through this assignment. The church does not need to tear itself down without realizing that Christ is the One who lifts us up. While the church may have failed, Christ still forgives and offers the second chance.

The apostle John records a story in his Gospel when Jesus encountered a woman caught in adultery. John 8:10–11 records, "When Jesus stood up, he said to her, 'Woman, where are they? Has no one condemned you?' 'No one, Lord,' she answered. 'Neither do I condemn you,' said Jesus. 'Go, and from now on do not sin anymore.'"

Go and do not sin anymore. That is the message to the church. Christ does not bring a word of condemnation to the church, but one of hope. A key aspect of identity is for the church to recognize who it is in the eyes of Christ. A good study through which the church needs to be taken is an examination of the book of Ephesians, noting every time it mentions who believers are in Christ. This type of study will bring balance to the discouraging aspects of false identity with the deep encouragement of the believer's identity in Christ. When a church knows and embraces its identity, both good and bad, it is on the path to revitalization.

CHAPTER 13

Rethink Vision

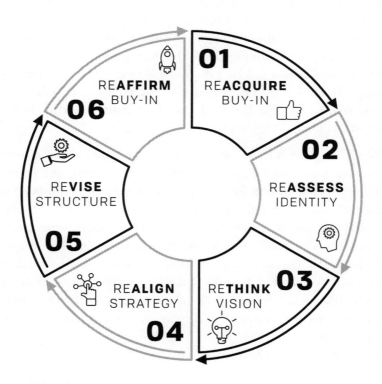

W hen a church reaches the point that it can rethink its vision, it is able at that point to literally start over. This step toward revitalization offers the opportunity for the church to reconnect with its biblical purpose and then begin to apply that vision to the church, the community, and the present culture. George Barna offers this definition of vision: "Vision for ministry is a clear mental image of a preferable future imparted by God to His chosen servants and is based upon an accurate understanding of God, self and circumstances."[1] Andrew Davis has cautioned church leaders to make sure that, in revitalization, they depend on the Word of God and not techniques. He has rightly said:

> The powerful Word of God has been building Christ's kingdom since the beginning of redemptive history. It has never been defeated, and it never will be. Satan has been opposing God's Word since he slithered up to Eve in the Garden of Eden and questioned God's authority, recruiting humanity through Adam to join his rebellion. . . . And the Word of God alone will revitalize a church if it is to be revitalized. The more the revitalizing leaders trust the Word of God alone, the more powerful their efforts will be.[2]

While the Bible is replete with principles, and one can glean incredible wisdom from watching other churches, do not miss the point of depending on God's Word. Everything that is done in revitalization must be biblically based. Though we speak of it in principle and in example, everything that the church now does must find its root in Scripture.

This fact is especially true as the church moves to develop a new vision. Regardless of how the church was birthed, how the church moved through its Life Stages, or how the church reached a position of decline, it now has the chance to start over. Its history is not forgotten, and its founders are not disparaged, but the church has a bright future as it rethinks vision.

Again, Davis has spoken well of this perspective:

> Visionary leadership is vital in all churches in order for them to bear maximum fruit for the glory of God. But it is especially essential in church revitalization situations. Such a church is overwhelmed. It has a track record of increasing weakness, a downward spiral of dwindling fruitfulness. Many of the godly members may feel powerless, aimless, and hopeless. They have lost their sense of mission and, what is far worse, their sense of God's greatness. Perhaps some unregenerate members have won the day in defining what the church is and does, leading to that

downward spiral. Though visionary leadership would be essential
even if that church were flourishing, never has there been so great
a need for leaders to step forward and cast a biblical vision for
what God is calling them to become and how he is commanding
them to obey.[3]

Scores of books exist that can help better define what vision is and
how it differs from a mission statement, so I am not going to revisit
those definitions at length here. Depending on the author, numerous
explanations and descriptions of vision surface, so much so, that vision
can be confusing.[4] For some, it is a general statement of the future that
the church desires to embrace. For others, vision encompasses specific-
ity, even including numerical goals within the vision. Many will include
the idea of a mission statement with the vision statement. Tony Morgan
makes this distinction between mission and vision:

> Mission . . . defines the primary purpose for the church.
> Typically, in twelve words or less . . . the church develop[s] a
> mantra that answers the why question. Why do we exist? . . .
> The vision . . . paints a picture of where the church is going in
> the future . . . develop[ing] that vision for three to five years out
> . . . it includes actual numerical targets. Other times it names a
> specific initiative that the church hopes to complete.[5]

Whatever process the church chooses for its revitalization, it is critical
that the church has designated time to rethink vision. Do not shorten the
time it takes to create a new vision for the church. Everything else develops out of this understanding of God's plan for the church. As strategic as
a church plant is in going through this process, so should the ReClaimed
Church be as it takes the proper steps toward revitalization. Now is the
time for a restart. Do not take this action lightly.

I like how Chuck Lawless addresses the problem of vision. How does
a church know when it does not have any vision? Notice what Lawless
suggests:

- Nobody, beginning with the leaders, can state the vision.
- Leadership tends to be reactive rather than proactive.
- Leaders are often divided.

- Ministries are disorganized and siloed.
- Passions rather than planning ignite the church's varied ministries.
- Internal conflict festers.
- The goal seems to be to "get through the next weekend" rather than to maximize efforts to reach the unchurched.
- Budget expenditures are a big deal.
- Many church members just sit.
- Strong leaders don't stay long.[6]

Spend time asking and answering the question: Where is the church going in the future? Through the mission statement, the church defines its primary purpose. Through its vision statement, it clarifies that mission into goals that are measurable and specific. Ultimately, the vision should magnify a powerful work of God.

Here are some examples:

Moses' Vision Statement for Israel

For the LORD your God is bringing you into a good land, a land with streams, springs, and deep water sources, flowing in both valleys and hills; a land of wheat, barley, vines, figs, and pomegranates; a land of olive oil and honey; a land where you will eat food without shortage, where you will lack nothing; a land whose rocks are iron and from whose hills you will mine copper. When you eat and are full, you will bless the LORD your God for the good land he has given you. (Deut. 8:7–10)

Saddleback Community Church (from *The Purpose Driven Church*)

It is the dream of a place where the hurting, the depressed, the frustrated, and the confused can find love, acceptance, help, hope, forgiveness, guidance, and encouragement.

It is the dream of sharing the Good News of Jesus Christ with the hundreds of thousands of residents in south Orange County.

It is the dream of welcoming 20,000 members into the fellowship of our church family—loving, learning, laughing, and living in harmony together.

It is the dream of developing people to spiritual maturity through Bible studies, small groups, seminars, retreats, and a Bible school for our members.

It is the dream of equipping every believer for a significant ministry by helping them discover the gifts and talents God gave them.

It is the dream of sending out hundreds of career missionaries and church workers all around the world, and empowering every member for a personal life mission in the world. It is the dream of sending our members by the thousands on short-term mission projects to every continent. It is the dream of starting at least one new daughter church every year.

It is the dream of at least fifty acres of land, on which will be built a regional church for south Orange County—with beautiful, yet simple, facilities including a worship center seating thousands, a counseling and prayer center, classrooms for Bible studies and training lay ministers, and a recreation area. All of this will be designed to minister to the local person—spiritually, emotionally, physically, and socially—and set in a peaceful, inspiring garden landscape.[7]

Eric Geiger and Kevin Peck suggest a very similar process for managing and changing the culture of the church. They encourage leadership to assess the church culture or, in other words, reassess identity.[8] Geiger and Peck then recommend, "Once the church culture is assessed, the hard work really begins. The leadership of the local church must take the next, daring step: casting a new vision for a healthy culture that makes disciples and reproduces leaders . . . culture change through vision-casting in the local church often means walking the church through corporate repentance."[9]

Will Mancini has captured one of the best ideas about vision. Mancini presents the concept of vision through the analogy of looking at a portrait. The picture has a foreground, midground, background, and beyond-the-horizon. Each of these sections allows for the execution of a vision that has parts that can be accomplished quickly but also encompass a vision for the future. Mancini describes vision in this manner:

1. **The foreground vision contains up to four specific initiatives that must be started within ninety days, as needed.** It clarifies weekly action steps and daily priorities for leaders, sequences short-term projects, tasks, and goals, and provides regular, positive accountability for individuals and teams.

2. **The midground vision is a single emphasis stated as both a qualitative and quantitative goal in the next year.** It generates excitement for what God is doing in the next year, focuses the attention, prayers, and resources of the church in a dramatic way, and reveals progress for celebration or recalibration.

3. **The background vision contains four ideas, primarily qualitative, that clarify the four most strategic emphases in the next three years in order to fulfill the beyond-the-horizon vision.** It creates a broad-level road map to approach the future, directs long-term allocation of church resources, and limits blind spots that would inhibit growth.

4. **The beyond-the-horizon vision is a vivid picture of the church's future five to twenty years away depending on the life stage and context of the church.** It shapes the destiny of the whole congregation, creates deeper meaning for individuals, and guides the development of long-term strategy.[10]

Additionally, Mancini offers these challenges that often arise to creating and implementing vision:

1. You craft a vision statement, but it's not meaningful enough to talk about after it's been written.
2. You articulate vision without defining the time frames involved.
3. When you do create goals, you create too many and try to do too much.

4. People who like to dream and people who like to execute are rarely on the same page.
5. People don't see the vision as pertinent to their ministry area.
6. The planning tool is so complicated that few people want to revisit it.
7. The vision rarely creates an exciting organizational focus.
8. The plan is too rigid and can't account for changes in the ministry environment.
9. The planning events happen randomly (not rhythmically) with little follow-up.
10. People can resist being accountable for goals.[11]

The purpose of spending so much time on rethinking vision is because vision clarifies the direction that the church will now take. What has happened in the past is irrelevant, because the church embraces a clear, compelling vision from God and a reason for their existence as a church. This vision, when correctly established and communicated, can impact every part of the church, including mission, leadership, people, stewardship, energy, faith, and ministry.[12] Malphurs and Penfold offer this reminder about vision:

It challenges believers to look beyond the pain and the mundane. It constantly holds out a picture of what could be. When we focus on Christ and his vision for us—his church—we find that we're able to rise above the ministry pain and mundane. Christ's vision holds out a wonderful picture of hope and invites us to hang in there spiritually. It's a wonderful story with a happy ending, and we must never forget that, especially when ministry seems impossible.[13]

> The purpose of spending so much time on rethinking vision is because vision clarifies the direction that the church will now take.

Do not underestimate the importance of vision. Read how others define vision and apply vision. Take time to develop a clear and compelling reason for why the church exists, where it is headed, and what the future holds for it. That vision will propel the church beyond its past mistakes and back into a viable life.

CHAPTER 14

Realign Strategy

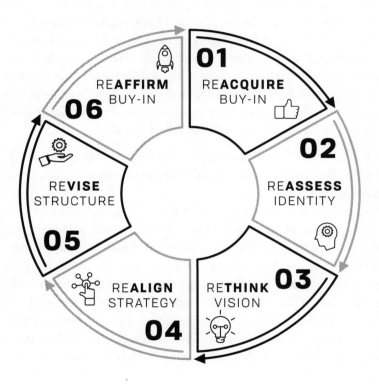

S trategy takes the vision and mission and puts them into practice. Vision is the *who* of the church. Strategy is the *how*. It is not independent of the vision but flows out of it. So often churches develop mission and vision statements but never determine anything from them. They put them on walls and in brochures, but the church never has a plan

for how to accomplish its vision, mission, or goals. The development of a
strategy is the next essential step to revitalization. J. D. Payne offers this
helpful explanation:

> So, what is strategy as related to the growth of the church?
> C. Peter Wagner defined strategy as "the chosen means to
> accomplish a predetermined goal." Aubrey Malphurs noted that a
> strategy is "the process that determines how you will accomplish
> the mission of the ministry." In the highly practical resource *The
> Church Planter's Toolkit*, Robert E. Logan and Steven L. Ogne
> commented that strategy is that process which translates vision
> into reality. Therefore, in light of these definitions, I have chosen
> to define strategy as *a prayerfully discerned, Spirit-guided process
> of preparation, development, implementation, and evaluation of the
> necessary steps involved in biblical church planting.*[1]

While Payne specifically applies strategy to church planting, his
definition fits well since revitalization is the opportunity for the church
to replant itself.

Many mission statements will involve the components of worship,
evangelism, and discipleship. Vision statements will include a lengthy
explanation of how the church envisions its future impact on the community and the world. Strategy, then, puts onto paper the plan for accomplishing that vision. Keep the strategy simple. A church that is restarting
does not need all the things it had when it was much larger. Mark Clifton
explains, "A replanted church must become a focused church. That refo-
cused, simplified church looks different in every context. You will need
to determine what your church's priorities look like as you strive to make
disciples in your context."[2]

Here is how a strategic plan works:

1. Develop a Strategic Leadership Team that establishes the vision
   and mission statement of the church. Do not complicate this
   process.
2. Examine the church's history and membership/attendance/giv-
   ing, along with the community's demographics.
3. Evaluate the church's strengths and weaknesses based on the
   information gathered.

4. Out of the vision and mission statements, determine:
   a. How will the church implement and define evangelism/outreach?
   b. How will the church accomplish and define discipleship/spiritual formation?
   c. How will the church provide and define worship?
   d. How will the church offer and define ministry/inreach?
   e. How will the church provide and define fellowship/community?
   f. How will the church develop and define stewardship?
   g. How will the church attract and define new members?
   h. How will the church ensure and define operation/facility effectiveness?
5. Under each of these eight categories:
   a. Set goals that are specific, measurable, and attainable
   b. Show the benefits of each goal
   c. Detail possible obstacles and how they can be overcome
   d. List action steps for accomplishing the goal
6. Get the congregation involved in affirming and implementing this strategy.[3]

Within the strategy, incorporate and remember these five principles. The strategy must be:

1. *Biblically Based.* Without the strategy being grounded in the Scriptures, churches risk deviating from Christ's vision for them.
2. *Stewardship Oriented.* A part of revitalization is being wise stewards of money, time, and people. Is this strategy advocating a healthy use of the church's assets to reach the world?
3. *Contextually Relevant.* Strategies must facilitate the connection between the people and the gospel. How will the church become the body of Christ in the community?
4. *Structurally Adaptable.* Strategy must be flexible and must be open to change.
5. *Reproducible.* The goal of revitalization is for the revitalized church to become a sponsoring church. Can the principles and practices followed be reproduced in other contexts and churches?[4]

By the time that a church reaches the downward spiral that demands that it revitalize, it probably is spending most of its time solving problems and casting blame. The church has lost its strategy because it has forgotten its vision. Reestablish a clear, compelling vision and lead the church to create and implement a strategy that allows it to restart. Regardless of where it was yesterday, realigning strategy redirects the church's energy away from complaint and into service.

Aubrey Malphurs offers this final thought:

Every church has a strategy that is partially reflected in its ministries and programs. The church must ask, Is this strategy a good one? Often a bad strategy does not have a vision or a mission to implement. It is easy to spot—people are going through the ministry motions, but not much is happening beyond maintenance.

A good strategy is the vehicle that enables the church to accomplish the mission (the Great Commission) and vision. The strategy moves the congregation from wherever they are spiritually (lost or saved) to where God wants them to be (mature). Therefore a good strategy delivers; that is, it helps the church accomplish the biblical mission that God has set for it.[5]

CHAPTER 15

Revise Structure

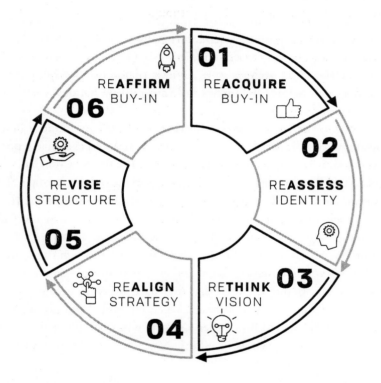

M ost, if not all, of the time churches reach the point of decline, they have an inadequate structure for that church and its context. Structure has been replaced by control and, therefore, it fails to accomplish the purpose of structure. Structure is intended to give a solid foundation for the vision, mission, and strategy. Robert Dale explains:

Organization gives the dream something to stand on and to work through. Organization lends muscular structure to churches. Structure is essential for form, strength, and purposeful life. Formal organization exists to do work, to pursue ministry goals. Informal organization emerges to meet needs. Whether formal or informal, structure helps congregations do their work "decently and in order" (1 Cor. 14:40).[1]

The ReClaimed Church must comprehend that, throughout this entire process from beginning to end, *everything is on the table.* No sacred cows remain, and no response is ever given for keeping or doing something simply because "we've always done it that way," or "we've never done it that way before." Churches fall into decline because they have poor structure.

One of my staff, when he was moving to our office, found a home that he and his family loved. It was just the right size and even had a pool. When they did the inspection, they found that the main beam that held the house together in the crawl space was so eaten out by termites that the inspector was afraid to crawl under it to inspect the rest of the floor joists. Needless to say, they did not buy the house because it had a terrible foundation.

Churches will make the fatal mistake of working through the steps of establishing new vision, new mission, and even new strategy, and then try to force these things into the ways that they have always done them. Even Jesus cautioned about such foolishness, when He said, "And no one puts new wine into old wineskins. Otherwise, the wine will burst the skins, and the wine is lost as well as the skins. No, new wine is put into fresh wineskins" (Mark 2:22).

The purpose of good structure is to align the church with effectiveness, not just efficiency. Structure that leads to decline is usually a control structure that becomes incredibly complicated and inefficient. Power groups emerge that dominate the resources and decisions, while other ministries begin to struggle for survival. This control eventually moves the church from a plateau into decline, because this type of structure actually stymies growth. It takes

> The purpose of good structure is to align the church with effectiveness, not just efficiency.

an act of congress to buy a box of pencils, because it must pass through every power committee in the church. The process in place is not for communication but for control.

When the church goes through revitalization, the time is ripe to address those problems and put the church in a position not just to solve the problems, but to prevent this type of situation from happening again. James Emery White offers some excellent suggestions at this point for developing an effective church structure:

> **Most decisions can be, and usually are, made by those leading that specific ministry.** If you have to work through committees or other bodies that are separate from the ministry itself, not only are bad decisions more prone to be made, but uninformed barriers can be erected for doing what needs to be done.
>
> **Staff/team leaders are allowed to build their own teams.** If a leader can't build [his/her] their own team, but someone or some group builds it for them, you have a recipe for disaster. Personality conflicts, lack of chemistry, and more will become far more likely.
>
> **Policies and procedures are kept to a minimum.** I once read of a thirty-three-page government document on how to buy a hammer. It's much better to hire people you trust to buy hammers, and turn them loose.
>
> **Votes are rare.** Some churches vote on everything from the color of the carpet to whether to add a new Sunday school class. The better structure is to vote on very few things, such as the annual budget or a new building, and let leaders lead.
>
> **There is an annual financial audit along with strong internal controls regarding money.** The best structures let leaders lead, but have strong internal controls and outside accountability regarding money. Yet in most churches, it's the exact opposite. Leaders are kept on a short leash, but you could drive a truck through their financial controls.

Organizational charts are kept fluid and nimble. Peter Drucker used to say that with every 15–20 percent growth, an organization will need an entirely new structure. His point was that as a church grows and develops, matures and expands, it will need new levels of leadership, new channels of communication, and new processes and procedures.

Hierarchy is avoided. The latest wave of companies that have proven their effectiveness are less hierarchical and more organic (think Google or Apple). Rather than a Management Team or Board approach to decision-making or problem-solving, the goal is to get the right people around the table for each and every challenge. This creates an ever-changing dynamic to leadership, but one that ensures more effectiveness.[2]

With these thoughts in mind, several areas therefore exist that must be reevaluated in order for the church to revitalize. These include:

1. Ministry Structures. If the church determines that a part of the vision and mission is to minister to the church and to the community, it must decide:
   a. What balance will be given between inreach and outreach?
   b. What percentage of the church's income will go toward ministry (inreach)?
   c. How many people do these ministries require for implementation and maintenance?
   d. How will the ministry balance with all the other organizational structures?
   e. How will ministry effectiveness be determined and at what point is a ministry to be improved or replaced?
2. Organizational Structures. How will the church function to carry out its mission and ministry?
   a. Will it use committees or teams?
   b. How will they be elected or serve?
   c. What are the requirements for service?
   d. How deep should organization go?
3. Leadership/Governance Structures: How will the church be led, administered, and overseen? The church must decide:

a. What leadership structure best assists the church in accomplishing its mission and in avoiding the mistakes of the past?

b. How will power struggles be avoided in the future, and how will structure aid in this process?

c. What types of leaders are needed, and what will be their requirements?

d. How will the church accept members, and how will membership requirements be enforced?

e. How do the current constitution and by-laws help or hinder revitalization?

f. How will the church accomplish staffing?

g. What percentage of the budget goes toward salaries?

h. What policies and procedures are in place that are usable and which ones need changing?

i. How will the church make small decisions and significant decisions?

j. Who will determine how resources are allocated?

4. Discipleship/Evangelism Structures: How will the church lead members to maturity, service, and mission?

a. How will the church balance discipleship with evangelism?

b. How will money be allocated for each?

c. What structure will be used that best accomplishes the discipleship vision of the church?

d. What structure will be used that best accomplishes the evangelism vision of the church?

5. Fellowship Structures: How will the church create community among established members, new members, and recent attendees?

a. How will facilities play a role in fellowship?

b. How will discipleship structures play a role in fellowship?

In so many cases, churches are satisfied with being on a growth plane until someone makes a bad decision, a need goes unnoticed, or someone gets overlooked. When structure is not in place and not followed, these issues easily sidetrack a church. Therefore, it is essential that the church revitalization effort spends time establishing a clear and workable structure for the congregation. Unfortunately, when people get angry or get their feelings hurt, they often show up with a copy of the by-laws, the policies manual, and *Robert's Rules of Order* in hand. They usually forget their Bibles. Take time to structure the church biblically and practically so that the church does not fall back into control issues or into a maintenance mind-set. Structure is intended to aid the church in accomplishing its vision and mission, not hinder it. When it becomes a part of the revitalization process, it enhances the growth and success of the vision.

Tony Morgan emphasizes this need through research he conducted with growing churches and how they connected structure directly with their strategy. He reports:

Churches that have a structure built around a clear strategy for ministry are growing 50 percent faster than those that do not.

- Average attendance growth in churches with a structure built around a clear strategy for ministry: 12 percent.
- Average attendance growth in churches without a structure built around a clear strategy for ministry: 8 percent.[3]

Do not be shortsighted when revising structure. It will lay a foundation for the church so that it can fulfill its mission and vision and avoid the problems that led the church into plateau and decline.

CHAPTER 16

Reaffirm Buy-In

The first stage to get a church back on a growth plane is buy-in. The last stage is buy-in. Without the church being on board throughout the entire process, the exercise will be undermined. Therefore, once all of these stages are complete and a clear process for revitalization has been developed, the leaders of the church need to return to the congregation and receive affirmation that they are ready and willing to move forward with these decisions.

During any major change that a church undertakes, people will buy in to the changes at different stages and through different means of communication. Consider these levels of buy-in.

1. *The Visionary Adopters.* These are the people who first realize that the church is in need of revitalization and are ready to make the changes necessary to get the church back on a growth plane. They are ready to get involved and take the lead. They are the trailblazers who guide the church toward the first stage of buy-in.

2. *The Early Adopters.* They know the situation is dire, and once they understand the process, they help champion the cause. They will add good insight into the process of change. They will be key in helping the church decide what type of revitalization will be necessary and will help promote this process. They buy in when the need is first presented to the church.

3. *The Intermediate Adopters.* They are the ones that are more passive in how they support the move toward revitalization. They will be supportive once they fully understand the vision, strategy, and structure. They begin to buy in as they understand the integrity of the process.

4. *The Late Adopters.* They have stood on the sidelines throughout the process of developing vision, strategy, and structure, doubting if these changes are necessary or are possible. Some are caught up in the past and do not see the need for change. Others have lost hope that the church can revitalize, replant, or restart. They may come on board once they see the momentum move toward revitalization.

5. *The Never Adopters.* Unfortunately, there may be those who never accept the process of revitalization. Some of them want the church to stay the same. They may be major stakeholders or power brokers and have a misguided understanding of the work of the church. They resist change and would rather let the church die than lose their control. Others just do not believe that there is hope for the church. Some are convinced that they are too old or too set in their ways to change. Some of the Never Adopters will

be antagonistic toward revitalization; others will be neutral and unsupportive, but will not stand in the way of change.

It would be nice to say that, at this point, the church will be in perfect unity and unanimity. There will be those who will be a part of the Early or Intermediate Adopters who will decide to step away. Others may never accept the process and will leave the church. It is interesting to see how different people handle difficult decisions. I listened to members of one church oppose relocation, wanting the church to stay where it was. When the church voted to relocate, they left the church, essentially relocating themselves. It was an indelible oxymoron.

Statistics and process offer a constant, but the one illogical, uncontrollable irregularity is people. I offer that word of counsel because it is so easy to become discouraged throughout the revitalization endeavor. Church leadership can do everything as clearly and as succinctly as possible, with every reason given, explored, and defended, and some people will still be resistant or opposed. This fact is true both in ecclesiological and professional situations. John Kotter and Lorne Whitehead offer a corporate look at the resistance to change in their book, *Buy-In*:

> Research clearly shows that people, even experienced executives, are not very good at transformational change, or change of any significance. Multiple studies have shown that 70 percent of the time, when significant change is needed, people back away, go into denial, try but fail rather miserably, or stop, exhausted, after achieving half of what they want using twice the budgeted time and money.[1]

When a church decides to make a significant change, personalities among the participants become very visible and volatile. Kotter and Whitehead humorously say that every committee (or church) saddled with the responsibility to engage, embrace, and initiate change is made up of the following personalities and people:

- Pompus Meani
- Avoidus Riski
- Allis Welli
- Divertus Attenti

- Heidi Agenda
- Spaci Cadetus
- Lookus Smarti
- Bendi Windi
- Your brother-in-law Hank
- And you[2]

Therefore, take the time to achieve enough buy-in at the beginning to lead the church through the stages of revitalization. It might be advisable to even think through those personality types, or the actual personalities that exist in the church, and work through ways that the church leadership can communicate with them, deal with their possible reasons for resistance, and curb any potential conflict in order to reach and achieve buy-in from these possible personalities of opposition. Then, before the point of no return in making the decision, seek to gain final buy-in from the entire congregation.

Revitalization is costly, but it is worth the cost. Not everyone will be on board, but attempt to bring with those who are adopters as many as possible, as the church takes on the challenge of becoming a ReClaimed Church.

Conclusion

One of my staff members got ahold of some old lumber. He took the wooden planks, assembled them together using a tongue and groove process, and then cut the completed piece into the shape of a state. When I saw one of his finished samples, I immediately wanted one. That old lumber, when reclaimed, made a beautiful centerpiece for my office. ReClaim is possible.

Years ago, I committed a major part of my ministry to teaching and leading church revitalization. I am convinced that we must have a church planting movement explode in our nation and in our world. I am also convinced that, in order to be the most effective at church planting, we must see a movement among our established churches to get healthy, stay healthy, and plant healthy churches. Every church, at some point in its existence, will need to make changes so that it can stay on a growth plane. That concept is the process of ReClaimed Church. While it is true that too many pastors and leaders have given up on the established church, it is also true that too many churches are dying every day. Just this week, somewhere between sixty-seven and seventy-seven churches in North America had their final services on Sunday. It is time to reverse this trend. Engaging that reversal is the purpose of *ReClaimed Church*.

Thom Rainer offers some final thoughts that might be helpful for examining and considering when revitalization may be the only hope that a church has in order to survive and to thrive once again. What are the evidences for the need for a church to be ReClaimed? Rainer suggests:

1. Declining worship attendance
2. Decline in frequency of attendance of church members

3. Lack of joy and vibrancy in the worship services
4. Little evangelistic fruit
5. Low community impact
6. More meetings than ministry
7. Acrimonious business meetings
8. Very few guests in worship services
9. Worship wars
10. Unrealistic expectations of pastoral care[1]

If these or perhaps other detrimental characteristics are evident, the church is most probably headed toward a downward spiral, the death spiral. The trend of church closures, however, can be averted. The answer lies in church revitalization. Regardless of where a church is located, is on the life or death scale, or is in size, shape, or form, it is possible for it to become a ReClaimed Church.

Church and Community Assessment

A number of assessment tools are available in order for the potential revitalization pastor to evaluate his church and his community. This assessment is applicable both for the pastor of an established church and for a pastor considering taking on the task of revitalizing a church. I am including an extensive outline of questions that should be asked and be evaluated in order to determine the potential effectiveness and success of a revitalization effort. The purpose of the assessment tool is not necessarily to detour the pastor or church from taking on a revitalization effort but to inform them of potential obstacles and challenges.

Assessment Tool

I. Finance
   A. What is the average giving percentage of individuals?
   B. What is the average giving per family unit?
   C. What is the per capita weekly giving average?
      1. Previous year
      2. Last three years
      3. Last five years
   D. How much debt does the church have?
   E. How does the church manage its finances and communicate that process to the congregation?

F.   Is there any system of endowment or legacy giving in
     place?

II.   Planning/Goal Setting
        A.   Does the church have any kind of planning in place?
             1. To help the church know where it is going
             2. To help leaders develop a vision
             3. To better allocate resources
             4. To build teamwork
        B.   What is church's perspective on:
             1. Its mission
             2. Its purpose
             3. Its vision
             4. Its plan
        C.   Where is the church in its vision cycle?
        D.   Does the church have a mission/vision statement and how
             does it fit into the mission and purpose of the church?

III.   Growth Barriers
        A.   Who are the stakeholders (people with a vested interest) in
             the church?
             1. Who are the stakeholders in the church?
             2. Who are the stakeholders outside the church?
             3. What are the spiritual barriers—the spiritual
                 stakeholders?
        B.   What are the other barriers the church faces?
             1. Is there a financial recession?
             2. Is there a declining population base?
             3. Is there competition with other churches?
             4. Is the community highly resistant to the gospel?
             5. Is the community stable?

IV.   Structures in the Church
        A.   What fellowship structures and opportunities are there in
             the church?

B. What ministry structures and opportunities are there in the church?
C. What leadership/governance structures are there in the church?
   1. What structure is currently in place?
   2. What improvements could be made to this structure?
   3. What hindrances are present that will prevent revitalization and growth?
   4. Will the church/denomination be open to allowing any changes in leadership structure?
   5. What hindrances to church revitalization are present because of the current leadership structures?
   6. Are there any ways to work within the system, while at the same time, prevent the hindrances from affecting the church?
D. What organizational structures are there in the church?

V. Outreach/Evangelistic Approaches
   A. Are members more concerned about the lost than their own preferences and comfort?
   B. Is the church led to pray for lost persons?
   C. Are the members of the church open to reaching people who don't look or act like them?
   D. Do conflicts and critics zap the evangelistic energy of the church?
   E. Do small groups and Sunday school classes seek to reach lost persons within their groups?
   F. Is the leadership of the church evangelistic?
   G. Do the sermons regularly communicate the gospel?
   H. Are there ministries in the church that encourage members to be involved in evangelistic outreach and lifestyle?
   I. Have programs become ends in themselves rather than means to reach people?
   J. Is there any process of accountability for members to be more evangelistic?

VI.   Community Analysis
       A. How well does the church look like the community?
       B. How well does the church serve as an advocate for the
           community?
       C. Does the church have any healthy partnerships with other
           churches?

VII.   Mission/Vision
       A. How much is the church driven by mission rather than
           programming?
       B. Does the church have its own identity?
       C. Does the church know God's specific plan for it at this
           time?

VIII. Assimilation Effectiveness
       A. How well in your church does a new person do the
           following:
           1. Identifies with the goals of the church.
           2. Is regular in worship attendance and in attendance
               at special services (Heb. 10:25).
           3. Attends Communion and Sunday school regularly
               and has Bible reading and family devotions in the
               home (Acts 2:42).
           4. Attends some special functions of the congregation
               such as council meetings, church picnics, special
               workshops, and midweek services.
           5. Is growing spiritually (2 Pet. 3:18).
           6. Has affiliated with the congregation.
           7. Has six or more friends in the church.
           8. Has a task or role that is appropriate for his or
               her spiritual gift(s) (Rom. 12; 1 Cor. 12; Eph. 4;
               1 Pet. 4:10–11).
           9. Is involved in a fellowship group (Acts 2:42).
           10. Gives regularly and generously (1 Cor. 16:2).
           11. Tells others about the Lord and His church
               (Matt. 28:18–20; Acts 1:8).

B. How well overall does the church as a whole do the following:
   1. How effectively does the church attract guests and is there a culture to do so?
      a. Preach about and pray for new people to come to church.
      b. Provide opportunities for church members to invite their friends.
      c. Have a user-friendly website.
   2. What kind of follow-up does the church do with first-time guests?
      a. How does the church begin follow-up the moment a person steps onto the church campus?
      b. Has the church established intentional touches that minister to newcomers and communicate effectively the church's mission?
   3. How many connection points are available for new people?
      a. Does the church have a New Member/Church Information Class?
      b. What kind of small group ministry does the church have?
      c. What kind of service opportunities for both guests and members does the church provide?

IX. Perceptions/Attitudes
   A. What is the primary thought of the church about itself?
   B. What is the primary perspective held by the community about the church?

X. Data and Statistical Analysis
   A. What is the worship attendance over the past five years?
   B. What is the small group Bible study attendance over the past five years?
   C. What are the budget receipts and expenditures over the past five years?

    D. What other statistical information is there that would help?

XI.   Demographic Assessment
    A. The church rolls:
        1. Where do the church members live?
        2. What is the age of the membership?
        3. What are the marital statuses of the congregation?
        4. What is the median income of the congregation?
        5. What is the educational level of the congregation?
    B. The church demographics:
        1. How many small groups does the church have, where do they meet, and what is their purpose?
        2. How many new people have visited the church over the last year to two years?
    C. What are the community demographics?
        1. What are the population changes over the past five years and within a five-mile radius of the church?
        2. What are the changes in the housing within a five-mile radius of the church?

XII.   Small Group/Sunday School
    A. Is there adequate space for present and future growth?
    B. Do class sizes match room sizes?
    C. What is the quality of the educational facilities?
    D. Are new units being created?
    E. What is the quality of teaching and how much time is allocated for teaching?
    F. What type of curriculum strategy is in place?
    G. How is the small group organized?
        1. Does each class have a teacher and assistant teacher?
        2. Is there a fellowship leader?
        3. Is there a process for ministry within and outside the class?
        4. Are records kept and does the class follow up with members?

5. Is there an outreach/evangelism leader?
6. Is there a prayer leader?
H. How does the staff relate to the Sunday school?
   1. Is it a priority of the pastor?
   2. Does the staff have responsibilities within the Sunday school?
   3. Does the staff attend Sunday school?
   4. How often and how well are volunteers recognized and rewarded?
I. How does the Sunday school secure new teachers and do teacher training?
J. What lines of accountability are in place?

XIII. Worship Issues
   A. What is the primary worship style?
   B. What worship wars has the church experienced or is experiencing?
   C. How well does the church actually worship?
   D. What is (are) the primary emphases of the worship experience?

XIV. Prayer Emphasis
   A. How well does the staff pray together?
   B. What prayer opportunities are offered to the church?

XV. Missions
   A. Does the church have a mission plan and vision in place?
   B. How well does the church see itself as a Great Commission church?
   C. Does the church follow through with an Acts 1:8 strategy?

XVI. Facilities Analysis
   A. What is the overall condition of the church property?
   B. What is the condition of the nursery and children's areas?
   C. What do the major hallways communicate?
   D. What does the primary church sign communicate?

E. How visible is the church property?

F. What is the condition of the most frequently used women's restroom?

G. What is the condition of the worship center?

H. Where is the main entrance, is it visible, and is there adequate signage?

I. How visible is the directional church signage?

J. How assessable and available is church parking?

XVII. Theological Issues

A. Where does the church see itself theologically?

B. How does its theology affect its practice?

C. Is the church divided over theology?

XVIII. Ministry-Staff Alignment

A. Initial questions to consider:

1. Would the church be open to looking for God-called individuals to come in a bivocational capacity to help fill the voids?

2. What are the demographics of the church and what do these demographics necessitate regarding staffing?

3. What demographic group will provide the greatest potential for outreach?

B. The characteristics of a high performance team:

1. Is there a clear, common purpose?

2. Are there crystal-clear roles?

3. Is there accepted leadership?

4. What are the effective processes in place for accomplishing goals?

5. Are there solid, interpersonal relationships?

6. How well does the team communicate?

7. Is there a regular process in place for evaluating staff and staff goals?[1]

XIX. Leadership
   A. The Pastor
      1. Am I the right person to lead this church?
      2. Can I make the cultural adjustment to this congregation and community?
      3. Could I be a more effective leader in another church context?
      4. What type of church should I be leading?
   B. The Staff
      1. Who should be on the staff?
      2. What position should that person hold?
      3. Who does not need to be on the staff?
      4. What is the calling of this person?
      5. Who will be affected by this person's change in position or departure?
      6. What is gained or lost in making this decision?

APPENDIX B

Church Revitalization Plan

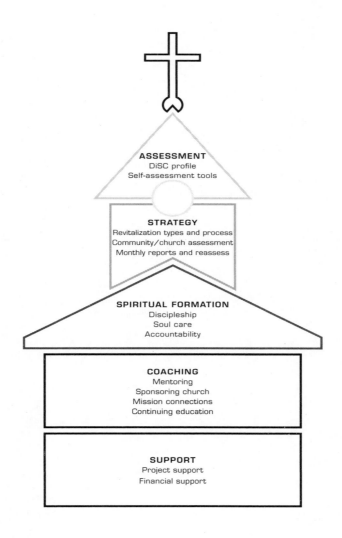

ASSESSMENT
DiSC profile
Self-assessment tools

STRATEGY
Revitalization types and process
Community/church assessment
Monthly reports and reassess

SPIRITUAL FORMATION
Discipleship
Soul care
Accountability

COACHING
Mentoring
Sponsoring church
Mission connections
Continuing education

SUPPORT
Project support
Financial support

Revitalization Steps

APPENDIX D

Stages of Life

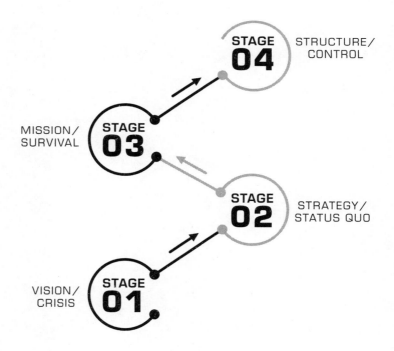

STAGE **04** — STRUCTURE/ CONTROL

MISSION/ SURVIVAL — STAGE **03**

STAGE **02** — STRATEGY/ STATUS QUO

VISION/ CRISIS — STAGE **01**

Stages of Death

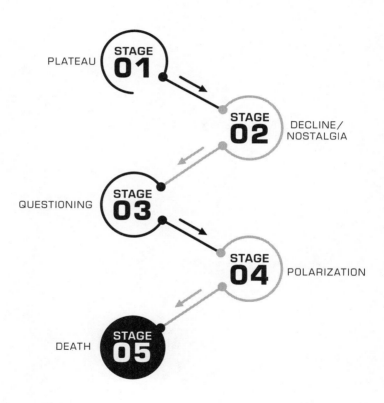

Life Stage Chart

	GROWING	PLATEAUED	DECLINING
VISION	FUTURE	PRESENT	PAST
STRATEGY	DOING STAGE	STATUS QUO	NO PLAN
MINISTRY	TO THE COMMUNITY	FOR THE CONGREGATION	FOR CONTROL GROUP
MISSION	GREAT COMMISSION	PROGRAM	NO MISSION
STRUCTURE	FOUNDATION	MAINTENANCE	SELF-PRESERVATION
MOTIVATION	VISION	PROGRAMS	STRUCTURE
EMPHASIS	REACHING COMMUNITY	CONGREGATION	REMAINING MEMBERS
FAITH	HIGH-RISK FAITH	CAREFUL FAITH	PROTECTED FAITH
DECISIONS	FAITH DECISIONS	ANALYZED DECISIONS	FEARFUL DECISIONS
SERVICE	THROUGH GIFTING	THROUGH POSITION	BY AVAILABILITY
STEWARDSHIP	GENEROSITY	RESPONSIBILITY	SURVIVAL
LEADERSHIP	FRESH	ENTRENCHED	SURVIVING
GROWTH	PROFESSION OF FAITH	TRANSFER OF LETTER	NEGATIVE GROWTH

Strengthening and Sending Church Replanters/ Revitalizers through the Development of 12 Core Competencies[2]

Below are twelve basic competencies that a church replanter/revitalizer will need to be successful. Having twelve competencies makes a one-year development track ideal.

1. Personal Devotion

There is nothing man can do apart from God being at work in him. Jesus makes clear in John 15 all efforts apart from Him will amount to nothing. In an endeavor as critical as revitalizing/restarting a church, there's nothing more critical than the heart, devotion, and passion of the replanter. Love for the replant, love for the church, and love for the ministry is important, but may it always fall in the shadow of your love and pursuit of Christ.

Sample Discussion Questions

1. What individuals have been your primary influences as it relates to your personal walk with Christ?
2. Describe a season in your life where you were thriving in your personal walk with the Lord. Share how your heart was filled with passion and a desire to know Jesus.
3. Interact with the following statement, "Pastors have wet eyes or a hard heart." Do you agree? If so, why? If not, why not?
4. Why is it so easy to become more focused on the work than upon your own heart? How have you fallen prey to this pitfall?
5. Consider the life of David in the Psalms. What can we learn about David's relationship with the Lord based on the various types of psalms recorded in the Bible?

Sample Action Plans

1. Write out your current pattern for spiritual development, enrichment, and growth. Share with a mentor. What needs to change? What needs to be supplemented?
2. Develop a plan for a new believer that will lead him or her to encounter God daily and begin growing as a Christian.
3. Describe your prayer life in detail. What do you pray about? Why do you pray? How long do you pray? Are you focused more on intercession than worship? What drives your prayers?

Recommended Resources

Dangerous Calling by Paul Tripp

The Minister as Shepherd by Charles Jefferson

Dynamics of Spiritual Life by Richard F. Lovelace

Transforming Prayer by Daniel Henderson

Can These Bones Live? by Bill Henard

2. Call to Ministry

What is the difference between the call that every Christian has to "minister" and the call that a select few have to "the ministry"? The Bible is clear that God calls some to serve the church through preaching, teaching and pastoral ministries (Acts 13:2, 20:28; Rom. 10:15; Eph. 4:11). As those who are pursuing this type of ministry, it is imperative to clarify that call and respond properly.

Discussion Questions

1.
2.
3.
4.
5.

Action Plans

1.
2.
3.

Recommended Resources

> *Discerning Your Call to Ministry* by Jason K. Allen
>
> *Dangerous Calling* by Paul David Tripp
>
> *Is God Calling Me?* by Jeff Iorg

3. Bibliology

God's Word is truth (John 17:17). Scripture is inspired by the Holy Spirit (2 Pet. 1:21), God-breathed, and thereby true, infallible, profitable for teaching, instruction, correction (2 Tim. 3:16), and sanctifying into maturity (John 17:17) and stands alone as highest authority, the truth by which all other claims of truth must be evaluated. Therefore, our lives, mission, and ministry must be tethered to the unchanging truth of God.

Discussion Questions

1.
2.
3.
4.
5.

Action Plans

1.
2.
3.

Recommended Resources

Taking God at His Word by Kevin DeYoung

The Inspiration and Authority of the Bible by B. B. Warfield

Peculiar Glory by John Piper

Grasping God's Word by J. Scott Duvall and J. Daniel Hays

Christ-Centered Preaching by Bryan Chapell

Revitalize by Andrew Davis

The Baptist Faith and Message by Charles Kelley, Richard Land, and Albert Mohler

4. Relationship Building

It is clear in Scripture that we have been created for relationship. This action begins with the mutual love, communication, and working of the Father, Son, and Holy Spirit. God then creates man, and immediately shows the need for us to be in proper God-glorifying relationships. Jesus talked about this many times in His teaching: "You shall love your neighbor as yourself" (Matt. 22:39 ESV), "Let your light shine before others" (Matt. 5:16 ESV), "No longer do I call you servants . . . but I have called you friends" (John 15:15 ESV).

Discussion Questions

1.
2.
3.
4.
5.

Action Plans

1.
2.
3.

Recommended Resources

The Art of Neighboring Jay Pathak and Dave Runyon

Making Friends for Christ by Wayne McDill

Life on Mission by Dustin Willis and Aaron Coe

5. Family

The family was designed by God as a reflection both of the essence of the gospel and our Triune God, within whose persons exists in onto-logical equality yet is diverse in role and function (Eph. 5:31–32; Gen. 1:26–27). From the creation order, men are the heads of their families, expressing this sacrificial headship through provision and responsible leadership, reflecting the cruciform love of Jesus toward His church (1 Tim. 2:13; 1 Cor. 11:3; Eph. 5:23, 25–30; Gen. 2:15; 1 Tim. 5:8). Wives are life-giving helpers who reflect the joyful submission of the church toward Jesus (Eph. 5:22–24; Gen. 2:18–22; 3:20). Through this mystery, the gospel is proclaimed in marriage.

Discussion Questions

1.
2.
3.

4.

5.

Action Plans

1.

2.

3.

Recommended Resources

What Did You Expect? by Paul Tripp

Love that Lasts by Gary and Betsy Ricucci

The Meaning of Marriage by Timothy and Kathy Keller

Marriage and the Mystery of the Gospel by Ray Ortlund Jr.

Gospel-Centered Family by Tim Chester

Foundations for Biblical Manhood and Womanhood by Wayne Grudem

God, Marriage, and Family by Andreas Köstenberger

The Church-Planting Wife by Christine Hoover

Helper by Design by Elyse Fitzpatrick

6. Church Planning/Administration

Trying to outline a system and structure for administration, planning, and strategy development can be as complicated and as complex as the individual who's developing the system and structure. It's important to remember that from a biblical perspective, God has given the work of the ministry to the church. Ephesians 4:12 calls pastors and planters to equip the saints for *the work of ministry.* In order to accomplish this Herculean effort, a clear definition is in order. Charles Tidwell rightly states, "Church administration is the leadership which equips the church to be the church and to do the work of the church. It is the guidance provided by church leaders as they lead the church to use its spiritual, human, physical, and financial resources to move the church toward reaching its objectives and fulfilling its avowed purpose. It is enabling the children of God who comprise the church to become and to do what they can become and do, by God's grace."[3]

Discussion Questions

1.
2.
3.
4.
5.

Action Plans

1.
2.
3.

Recommended Resources

How to Lead and Still Have a Life by H. Dale Burke

Deliberate Church by Mark Dever and Paul Alexander

Designed to Lead by Eric Geiger and Kevin Peck

Center Church by Tim Keller

The Unity Factor by Larry Osborne

7. Missiology

God's primary vehicle for expanding His kingdom is the church. God's people loving Him and loving others will drive the mission of God in the world. The church, functioning properly, will forcefully push back the darkness and continue to send men and women into the mission field (Matt. 16:18; Acts 13:3). The result will be new Christians and new churches.

Discussion Questions

1.
2.
3.
4.
5.

Action Plans

1.
2.
3.

Recommended Resources

The Spontaneous Expansion of the Church by Roland Allen

Radical by David Platt

Reaching and Teaching by David Sills

Gaining by Losing by J. D. Greear

Through Gates of Splendor by Elisabeth Elliot

Mountain Rain: A Biography of James O. Frase Pioneer Missionary to China by Eileen Crossman

Apostolic Church Planting by J. D. Payne

Small Town Jesus by Donnie Griggs

8. Discipleship

It is through disciples making disciples that people meet Jesus, grow in the grace and knowledge of Jesus, and engage in the very mission of Jesus. Every Christian should seek other Christians who are advanced in maturity, to learn from spiritually and practically, while seeking out Christians younger in the faith or maturity, for whom to encourage, instruct, and pray (Prov. 27:17; 1 Cor. 4:14–17; 11:1; Phil. 3:17; Deut. 11:18–19; Acts 2:42).

Discussion Questions

1.
2.
3.
4.
5.

Action Plans

1.
2.
3.

Recommended Resources

Multiply: Disciples Making Disciples by Francis Chan

The Cost of Discipleship by Dietrich Bonhoeffer

The Trellis and the Vine by Colin Marshal and Tony Payne

Total Church by Steve Timmis

Everyday Church by Steve Timmis

Gospel Coach by Scott Thomas

Spiritual Disciplines for the Christian Life by Donald Whitney

Leading, Teaching, and Making Disciples by Michael Mitchell

9. Emotional Stability

Statistically, the pastorate is one of the career fields that reports one of the highest number of those struggling with depression. Men who are leading local churches are often depressed. Why is this? It is an incredibly stressful job; one we must be prepared to undertake, or the stress will wreck our own minds and our families. Because of this fact, we must be well prepared to continually dwell in joy. In the spirit of Nehemiah, we exhort ourselves: "Do not grieve, because the joy of the LORD is [our] strength" (Neh. 8:10).

Discussion Questions

1.
2.
3.
4.
5.

Action Plans

1.
2.
3.

Recommended Resources

> *Note to Self* by Joe Thorn
>
> *It's Personal* by Brian Bloye
>
> *Crazy Busy* by Kevin DeYoung
>
> *How People Change* by Timothy Lane and Paul Tripp
>
> *Dangerous Calling* by Paul Tripp
>
> *Boundaries* by Henry Cloud and John Townsend

10. Visionary Perseverance

A church replanter/revitalizer must be a visionary who understands the stewardship of the church. He must have the qualities of loving the church, of loving multiple generations, and of having a commitment to longevity. Church turnaround is not a sprint; it is a marathon. Visionary perseverance requires the employment of the gifts, talents, and resources that the Master has given and using them in proper stewardship. It is seeing what others do not see and being faithful to keep to the task. Jesus said, "No one who puts his hand to the plow and looks back is fit for the kingdom of God" (Luke 9:62).

Discussion Questions

1.
2.
3.
4.
5.

Action Plans

1.
2.
3.

Resources

God Dreams by Will Mancini

Kingdom First by Jeff Christopherson and Mac Lake

The Man Who Thought Different by Karen Blumenthal

Planting Growing Churches by Aubrey Malphurs

Planting Missional Churches by Ed Stetzer

Autopsy of a Deceased Church by Thom Rainer

Biblical Church Revitalization by Brian Croft

Reclaiming Glory by Mark Clifton

11. Soteriology

Salvation, and the study of it, is one of the most important doctrines in the life of the church. Additionally, what a church replanter believes about salvation will dictate much of his practice as it relates to preaching, evangelism, mission work, and multiplication. The "who," "what," "when," "where," "why," and "how" of salvation should all be worked through and clearly articulated long before the work of replanting begins. Regardless of the theological camp out of which a replanter is birthed, he must do the biblical exegesis himself in order to have tightly held convictions that will guide, not just ministry and practice, but his own devotion to Christ as well.

Discussion Questions

1.
2.
3.
4.
5.

Action Plans

1.
2.
3.

Recommended Resources

What Is the Gospel? by Greg Gilbert

The Cross and Salvation by Bruce Demarest

The Death of Death in the Death of Christ by John Owen

All of Grace by Charles H. Spurgeon

12. Leadership

Leadership is a necessity among pastors, church planters, replanters, and revitalizers. People will look to a pastor for an example and for advice. The ability to lead is crucial and important, which is why Paul was able to say, "Imitate me, as I also imitate Christ" (1 Cor. 11:1). True Christian leadership minimizes the leader and exalts the Lord, recognizing that the ability to lead comes from God in the first place.

Discussion Questions

1.
2.
3.

4.

5.

Action Plans

1.

2.

3.

Recommended Resource

Everyday Church by Tim Chester and Steve Timmis

Church Unique by Will Mancini

Death by Meeting by Patrick Lencioni

100 Principles for Leadership by Brian Howard

The Conviction to Lead by Albert Mohler

Mistakes Leaders Make by Dave Kraft

Church Restart Covenant Agreement

This covenant agreement is between the Original Church, Church Restart, and Sending Church

1. This Covenant Agreement is in effect for 3½ years.
2. The Original Church and Sending Church will rejoice and honor the church's history. Before the Original Church shuts down, a final service of honor will be celebrated. The Original Church's history will not be forgotten or disparaged. Those in the Original Church commit, however, to a new beginning that looks to the future and not the past. The term "shut down" does not mean that the Original Church ceases to exist at that point but that it enters into the process of transitioning toward its new beginning. The Original Church is encouraged to meet in small groups with occasional times for corporate worship. Its primary focus, though, is on the development of its new constitution, vision, mission, structure, and future. The members are encouraged to give attention to personal discipleship, growth, and development for the new launch. The unchurched should be consistently invited to the small group Bible studies.
3. The Original Church enters into this covenant agreement with the Sending Church. The Sending Church commits to provide leadership, mentoring, coaching, and encouragement for the Church ReStart. This mentoring process includes, but is not

limited to, utilizing the 12 Competencies for developing the Church ReStart pastor.

4. A Transition Team will be established. This team will be comprised of individuals from the Sending Church and Original Church. Input will be sought and received from the state convention. The transition team will be empowered to make all decisions during the time of transition from when the Original Church shuts down and the Church ReStart is launched. The team will continue to function for at least the first year of the Church ReStart's launch.

   a. The Transition Team will develop a new mission statement, vision statement/goals, Constitution and By-Laws, strategies, and structure for the Church ReStart. Others in the Original Church and Sending Church can be included in these discussions.

   b. The Transition Team will be responsible for the recommendation of a new pastor, the acquisition of pulpit supply, and other leadership responsibilities. Care must be taken not to jump ahead of the ReStart process.

4. An assessment will be made for the potential and success of the Church ReStart at the Original Church's site and the community's perception of the Original Church. If it is determined that the Original Church's site is prohibitive to future growth, both the Original Church and Church ReStart agree to search for a more conducive meeting place. Any proceeds from properties sold will be used for the benefit of the Church ReStart. This assessment will also be utilized to provide insight into the development of mission, vision, strategy, and structure.

5. The Original Church will shut down for a predetermined period of time, at least for six months. A launch date will be set. The Original Church will reopen as the Church ReStart with a new name, new pastor, and new leadership. The purpose of this shut down is to allow for the Transition Team and Original Church to develop its necessary structure, to separate from the past, and to create a new DNA and identity for the Church ReStart.

Notes

Acknowledgments

1. From an email correspondence with Ken Priddy.

Introduction

1. Dictionary, https://www.google.com/#q=reclaim.

2. The term *Life Stage* is used interchangeably with other terms such as *Life Cycle* or *Bell Curve*. Different writers choose different ways to describe the stages a church travels through as it goes from birth to plateau to death.

3. See Robert D. Dale, *To Dream Again: How to Help Your Church Come Alive* (Nashville: Broadman Press, 1984).

4. Haddon Robinson, "The Heresy of Application," in *The Art and Craft of Biblical Preaching*, Haddon Robinson and Craig Brian Larson, gen. eds. (Grand Rapids: Zondervan, 2005), 306.

5. R. Albert Mohler Jr., "The Sheer Weightlessness of So Many Sermons— Why Expository Preaching Matters," http://www.albertmohler.com/2013/08/21 /the-sheer-weightlessness-of-so-many-sermons-why-expository-preaching-matters/.

Chapter 1

1. Richard R. Melick, *The New American Commentary, vol. 32, Philippians, Colossians, Philemon* (Nashville: Broadman and Holman Publishers, 1991), 139.

Chapter 2

1. George W. Bullard Jr., *Pursuing the Full Kingdom Potential of Your Congregation* (St. Louis, MO: Chalice Press, 2005), 76.

2. Aubrey Malphurs, *Advanced Strategic Planning: A New Model for Church and Ministry Leaders* (Grand Rapids: Baker Books, 1999), 150.

3. Tim Spencer explains, "The 80% Rule observes that churches will grow to fill their available space. Ken Hemphill coined the term "Bonsai Theory" to illustrate this principle. A bonsai tree grows to fill the pot in which it is planted, but it will never grow larger than its container. Churches grow in much the same pattern in several areas: Worship Service Space, Bible Study/Small Group Space, Parking Spaces, Nursery/Preschool Space. The 80% Rule says that a church will begin to plateau when it reaches 80% capacity in the spaces it has to grow.

Win Arn applies the rule with an 87:100 ratio, meaning that the plateau begins at 87% capacity. Whatever ratio you use, filling available space has a chilling effect on your church's growth potential." See Ministry Action Plans, "Church Growth Ratios," http://ministryactionplans.com/church-growth-ratios/.

4. Thom S. Rainer, *The Unchurched Next Door: Understanding Faith Stages as Keys to Sharing Your Faith* (Grand Rapids: Zondervan, 2003), 23.

5. Sam Rainer, "Why the Status Quo Is So Tempting (and Dangerous)," http://samrainer.com/2015/04/why-the-status-quo-is-so-tempting-and-dangerous/.

Chapter 3

1. See Bill Henard, *Can These Bones Live? A Practical Guide to Church Revitalization* (Nashville: B&H Publishing Group, 2015), 214–15.

2. John B. Polhill, *New American Commentary*, vol. 26, *Acts* (Nashville: Broadman Press, 1992), 183.

3. John F. MacArthur, *Acts 1–12*, in *The MacArthur New Testament Commentary* (Chicago: Moody Press, 1994), 231.

4. http://www.soc.duke.edu/natcong/.

5. http://hirr.hartsem.edu/research/fastfacts/fast_facts.html#sizecong.

Chapter 4

1. George W. Knight, The Pastoral Epistles, in *The New International Greek Testament Commentary* (Grand Rapids: Eerdmans, 1992), 9.

2. Mark Dever, *What Is a Healthy Church?* (Wheaton, IL: Crossway, 2007), 40.

3. D. G. Peterson, *Godliness*, in *New Bible Dictionary*, D. R. W. Wood, I. H. Marshall, A. R. Millard, J. I. Packer, and D. J. Wiseman, eds. (Downers Grove, IL: InterVarsity Press, 1996), 422.

4. John F. MacArthur, *1 Timothy*, in *The MacArthur New Testament Commentary* (Chicago: Moody Press, 1995), 164.

5. R. Kent Hughes and Bryan Chapell, *1 & 2 Timothy and Titus* (Wheaton, IL: Crossway, 2012), 129–30.

6. David W. Torrence and Thomas F. Torrence, eds., *1st and 2nd Timothy*, vol. 10 in *Calvin's Commentaries* (Grand Rapids: Eerdmans, 1964), 261.

7. Ibid., 263.

8. Lisa Cannon Green, "Research Finds Few Pastors Give Up on Ministry," http://www.lifeway.com/pastors/2015/09/01/research-finds-few-pastors-give-up-on-ministry/.

9. Brooks R. Faulkner, "Leaving-Why Ministers Are Leaving the Ministry," http://media.mobaptist.org/public/pastoral ministry/LEAVINGWhyMinisters_leave_ministry.pdf.

10. Ed Stetzer and Mike Dodson, *Comeback Churches: How 300 Churches Turned Around and Yours Can Too* (Nashville: B&H, 2007), 19.

11. Win Arn, *The Pastor's Manuel for Effective Ministry* (Monrovia, CA: Church Growth, 1988), 45.

12. Thom S. Rainer, *Breakout Churches: Discover How to Make the Leap* (Grand Rapids: Zondervan, 2005), 45.

13. Thom S. Rainer, "Dispelling the 80 Percent Myth of DecliningChurches," http://thomrainer.com/2017/06/dispelling-80-percent-myth-declining-churches/.

14. Ed Stetzer, "CP Study Part 2: How Many Church Plants Really Survive— And Why?," http://www.namb.net/namb1cb2col.aspx?id=8590001104.

15. Green, "Research Finds Few Pastors Give up on Ministry."

16. Arnold Kurtz, "The Pastor as a Manager of Conflict in the Church," *Andrews University Seminary Studies*, vol. 20 (1982), 112.

17. Quoted in Jim Wilson, "Church Conflict Can Prove Healthy If Handled Biblically, Speaker Says," http:// http://www.bpnews.net/702/church-conflict -can-prove-healthy-if-handled-biblically-speaker-says. The quotation comes from Lloyd Elder, professor and director of the Moench Center of Church Leadership at Belmont University, Nashville, TN.

18. Ken Sande, "Christian Conciliation Procedures," (Billings, MT: Institute for Christian Conciliation, 1993), 9.

19. Carl F. George and Robert E. Logan, *Leading and Managing Your Church: Effective Management for the Christian Professional* (Grand Rapids: Revell, 1987), 147–64.

20. For a more detailed account of this idea, see Bill Henard, *Can These Bones Live?*, 30–42.

21. Thom S. Rainer, "Autopsy of a Deceased Church," http://thomrainer .com/2013/04/24/autopsy-of-a-deceased-church-11-things-i-learned/. Rainer has also put these ideas into book form. See Thom S. Rainer, *Autopsy of a Deceased Church: 12 Ways to Keep Your Church Alive* (Nashville: B&H, 2014).

22. Adapted from The Institute for Christian Conciliation.

23. Said at a meeting at Bell Ave. Baptist Church, Knoxville, TN, in 1983.

24. "How Should Conflict in the Church Be Handled?," http://www.got questions.org/church-conflict.html.

25. Greg Sumii, "Preventing Unhealthy Church Conflict Resolution" (Fresno, CA: California Southern Baptist Convention, 2002), 6.

26. Glenn C. Daman, "When Sheep Squabble—Dealing with Conflict in the Smaller Church," *Enrichment Journal* (Spring 2005), 7–8.

27. Sande, "Christian Conciliation Procedures," 21.

28. Eric Reed, "Leadership Surveys Church Conflict," http://www. Christianity Today.com/go/conflict.

Chapter 5

1. Brian Dodd, "13 Reasons Churches Have Plateaued or Declining Attendance," http://briandoddonleadership.com/2016/07/10/13-reasons-churches -have-plateaued-or-declining-attendance/.

2. Derek Thompson, "What in the World Is Causing the Retail Meltdown of 2017?," https://www.theatlantic.com/business/archive/2017/04/ retail-meltdown-of-2017/522384/.

3. Aubrey Malphurs, "Ten Warning Signs of a Church Plateau," http:// www.malphursgroup.com/10-warning-signs-of-church-plateau/.

4. "Plateau," *Webster's Seventh New Collegiate Dictionary* (Springfield, MA: G & C Merriam Company, 1963), 649.

5. For example, from an internal analysis done by LifeWay, Cliff Tharp reports, "Information from the Annual Church Profile (ACP) was used in this preliminary analysis of the church growth of Southern Baptist churches. Southern Baptist churches complete the ACP annually. The latest information available at the time of this analysis was the 1998 data. Thus, 1993–1998 was the five-year span used to determine the growth category of churches." See Cliff Tharp, "Analysis of the Growth Status of Southern Baptist Churches," (2000).

6. Jeff Christopherson, "The Plateaued Congregation and the Lore of Church Growth," https://www.namb.net/send-network-blog/the-plateaued -congregation-and-the-lore-of-church-growth.

7. Chris Hefner, "8 Observations of a Revitalized Church," http://www. lifeway.com/pastors/2014/10/09/8-observations-about-a-revitalized-church/.

8. Ibid.

9. Thom S. Rainer, "Eight Common Characteristics of Successful Church Revitalizations," http://thomrainer.com/2015/05/eight-common-characteristics -of-successful-church-reVitalizations/.

10. Information gleaned from a lecture by Mark Clifton when he guest-lectured at a Doctor of Ministry seminar at The Southern Baptist Theological Seminary in January 2018.

11. Dale Burke, "Even Healthy Churches Need to Change," in *Leadership* (Fall 2005), 44, emphasis original.

12. Ibid., 44–46.

Chapter 6

1. Thom S. Rainer, "Is There a Church Death Spiral?," http://thomrainer .com/2017/07/church-death-spiral/.

2. Robert D. Dale, *To Dream Again: How to Help Your Church Come Alive* (Eugene, OR: Wipf and Stock Publishers, 2004), 16.

3. Ichak Adizes, *Corporate Lifecycles: How and Why Corporations Grow and Die and What to Do about It* (Paramus, NJ: Prentice Hall, 1988).

4. Ichak Adizes, "Adizes Corporate Lifecycle," http://adizes.com/lifecycle/. See https://www.adizes.com/pdf/lifecyclesoforg.pdf.

5. Ibid.

6. Harry Reeder, "The Present Hope of Church," http://www.ligonier.org /learn/articles/the-present-hope-of-the-church/.

7. Gary L. McIntosh, *There's Hope for Your Church: First Steps to Restoring Health and Growth* (Grand Rapids: Baker, 2012), 30.

8. Mark Clifton and Sam Parkison, "Is It Natural for a Church to Die?," vol. 2, *Replant Journal*, 20.

9. Mark Clifton, *Reclaiming Glory: Revitalizing Dying Churches* (Nashville: B&H Publishing Group, 2016), 22–30.

Chapter 7

1. R. Albert Mohler, "Christ Will Build and Rebuild His Church: The Need for 'Generation Replant,'" in *A Guide to Church Revitalization*, R. Albert Mohler, ed. (Louisville: SBTS Press, 2015), 10–11.

2. "The Top 20 Countries Where Christianity Is Growing the Fastest," https://discipleallnations.wordpress.com/2013/08/25/the-top-20-countries -where-christianity-is-growing-the-fastest/.

3. "Quick Facts about Global Christianity," http://www.gordonconwell .edu/ockenga/research/Quick-Facts-about-Global-Christianity.cfm#6.

4. Barry A. Kosmin and Ariela Keysar, "American Religious Identification Survey Summary Report" (Hartford, CT: Trinity College, 2009), i.

5. Mark Dever, *What Is a Healthy Church?* (Wheaton, IL: Crossway, 2007), 63.

6. Ibid., 63–120.

7. Tony Morgan, *The Unstuck Church: Equipping Churches to Experience Sustained Health* (Nashville: Thomas Nelson, 2017), 93–94.

8. Stephen A. Macchia, *Becoming a Healthy Church: 10 Traits of a Vital Ministry* (Grand Rapids: Baker Books, 1999), 215–22.

9. Morgan, *The Unstuck Church*, 120–21, emphasis original.

10. Ibid., 130–31.

11. Phil Stevenson, "Plateaued Church: Creating a Culture for Growth," in *The Great Commission Research Journal*, vol. 3, no. 2 (Winter 2012), 202–204, emphasis original.

12. Gary L. McIntosh, *Taking Your Church to the Next Level: What Got You Here Won't Get You There* (Grand Rapids: Baker Books, 2009), 56.

13. Gary L. McIntosh, *There's Hope for Your Church: First Steps to Restoring Health and Growth* (Grand Rapids: Baker, 2012), 52–53.

14. Robert D. Dale, *To Dream Again: How to Help Your Church Come Alive* (Eugene, OR: Wipf and Stock Publishers, 2004), 95.

15. McIntosh, *Taking Your Church to the Next Level*, 67–69.

Chapter 8

1. The idea behind this section originated with Kenneth E. Priddy, executive director of the GO Center and president of The Ken Priddy Group. I contacted Dr. Priddy and received permission to use this material without any exceptions or qualifications. Priddy's concept was originally published in *The Great Commission Research Journal.* See Kenneth E. Priddy, "Church Turnaround: Perspectives, Principles, and Practices," in *The Great Commission Research Journal,* vol. 3, no. 2 (Winter 2012), 161–76.

2. See Bill Henard, *Can These Bones Live? A Practical Guide to Church Revitalization* (Nashville: B&H Publishing Group, 2015), 47–55.

3. George Barna, *The Frog in the Kettle: What Christians Need to Know About Life in the Year 2000* (Ventura, CA: Regal Books, 1990), 21.

Chapter 9

1. John Maxwell, *The 21 Irrefutable Laws of Leadership: Follow Them and People Will Follow You* (Nashville: Thomas Nelson, 1998), 41.

2. *The Andy Griffith Show,* "Opie and the Spoiled Kid," Season 3, Episode 21, 1963.

3. For the church to "shut down" does not mean that it ceases to exist even for a period of time, but that it focuses on simplifying its work and ministry to prioritize small groups, personal growth, and the development of a strategy for the future. Every church needs to check local laws for incorporation, name changes, and bank statements. Most of the time, these steps should be easy to accomplish, but care should still be taken.

4. Kenneth O. Gangel, *Holman New Testament Commentary,* vol. 5, *Acts* (Nashville: B&H Publishers, 1998), 10.

5. Mark Clifton, *Reclaiming Glory: Revitalizing Dying Churches* (Nashville: B&H Publishing Group, 2016), 31.

6. From a personal conversation with J. D. Payne.

7. **Caution:** It must be cautioned here that the churches that provide support for a revitalization church must not engage in the work in such a way that its assistance actually hurts the revitalization church rather than helps it. Any project must demand that both churches participate in the event. Sponsoring churches should not come to the revitalization church and conduct Vacation Bible School, an evangelistic outreach, or a ministry project if the revitalization church is not directly involved in the project itself, both financially and with personnel. An important resource for understanding this requirement is Steve Corbett and Brian Fikkert's book, *When Helping Hurts: How to Alleviate Poverty Without Hurting the Poor and Yourself* (Chicago: Moody, 2009). Too many sponsoring or mission connection churches have hurt the revitalization process because they have not understood this principle. The purpose of the mission connection or sponsorship is not for the sponsoring church to feel good

about itself because it conducted a mission project, but to serve the revitalization church and help get it back on a growth plane. This fact cannot be emphasized strongly enough.

8. Harry L. Reeder III, *From Embers to a Flame: How God Can Revitalize Your Church* (Phillipsburg, NJ: P&R Publishing, 2008), 22.

Chapter 10

1. See https://www.discinsights.com/disc-profile-the-biblical-personality -system.html.

2. Thom S. Rainer, "Nine Questions You Should Ask Before Leading a Church Revitalization," http://thomrainer.com/2014/07/nine-questions-ask -leading-church-revitalization/.

3. Mark Clifton, *Reclaiming Glory: Revitalizing Dying Churches* (Nashville: B&H Publishing Group, 2016), 115–38.

4. A helpful book that details strengths for leadership is Tom Rath, *Strengths Finder 2.0* (New York: Gallup Press, 2007).

5. http://brefigroup.co.uk/coaching/coaching_and_mentoring.html.

6. Aubrey Malphurs and Gordon E. Penfold, *Re:Vision, The Key to Transforming Your Church* (Grand Rapids: Baker Books, 2014), 189.

7. Ibid., 192.

8. John C. Maxwell, "Leadership Is Influence: Nothing More, Nothing Less," http://www.christianitytoday.com/pastors/2007/july-online-only/090905.html.

9. John C. Maxwell, "The 5 Levels of Leadership," http://www.johnmax-well.com/blog/5-levels-of-leadership.

10. Quoted in John C. Maxwell, *The 21 Indispensable Qualities of a Leader: Becoming the Person Others Will Want to Follow* (Nashville: Nelson, 1999), 1.

Chapter 11

1. Bill Day, "Healthy, Growing Churches 2015 ACP Data," presentation for the Leavell Center for Evangelism and Church Health, New Orleans Baptist Theological Seminary, 2015.

2. John P. Kotter and Dan S. Cohen, *The Heart of Change: Real-Life Stories of How People Change Their Organizations* (Boston: Harvard Business School Publishing, 2002), xii.

3. These steps were adapted from Bruna Martinuzzi, "9 Ways to Get Others to Buy In on Change," https://www.americanexpress.com/us/small-business /openforum/articles/9-ways-to-get-others-to-buy-in-on-change/.

4. Tony Morgan, *The Unstuck Church: Equipping Churches to Experience Sustained Health* (Nashville: Thomas Nelson, 2017), 177–78.

Chapter 12

1. Carey Nieuwhof, "10 Things That Demonstrate the World You Grew Up in No Longer Exists," https://careynieuwhof.com/10-things-that-demonstrate -the-world-you-grew-up-in-no-longer-exists/?mc_cid=ccb131cd92&mc _eid=ff801f7502.

Chapter 13

1. George Barna, *The Power of Vision: How You Can Capture and Apply God's Vision for Your Ministry* (Ventura, CA: Regal Books, 1992), 28.

2. Andrew M. Davis, *Revitalize: Biblical Keys to Helping Your Church Come Alive Again* (Grand Rapids: Baker Books, 2017), 78.

3. Ibid., 105–106.

4. There is some distinction between definitions and application of the idea of vision between several authors. Compare George Barna, *The Power of Vision: How You Can Capture and Apply God's Vision for Your Ministry* (Ventura, CA: Regal Books, 1992); Tony Morgan, *The Unstuck Church: Equipping Churches to Experience Sustained Health* (Nashville: Thomas Nelson, 2017); Aubrey Malphurs and Gordon E. Penfold, *Re:Vision, The Key to Transforming Your Church* (Grand Rapids: Baker Books, 2014); Andrew M. Davis, *Revitalize: Biblical Keys to Helping Your Church Come Alive Ag*ain (Grand Rapids: Baker Books, 2017); and Will Mancini, *God Dreams: 12 Vision Templates for Finding and Focusing Your Church's Future* (Nashville: B&H Publishing Group, 2016).

5. Tony Morgan, *The Unstuck Church: Equipping Churches to Experience Sustained Health* (Nashville: Thomas Nelson, 2017), 52.

6. Chuck Lawless, "10 Signs That a Church Has No Clear Vision," http:// chucklawless.com/2017/03/10-signs-that-a-church-has-no-clear-vision/?utm _source=Blog+List&utm_campaign=9ac9840b94-Daily_Blog_Emails&utm _medium=email&utm_term=0_1f3938126f-9ac9840b94-100309145.

7. Aubrey Malphurs, *Advanced Strategic Planning: A New Model for Church and Ministry Leaders* (Grand Rapids: Baker Books, 1999), 328, 330–31. Note that Saddleback's vision statement was developed when they had twenty members.

8. Eric Geiger and Kevin Peck, *Designed to Lead: The Church and Leadership Development* (Nashville: B&H Publishing Group, 2016), 142.

9. Ibid., 143.

10. Will Mancini, "Your Next Big Dream: 12 Vision Templates to Find and Focus Your Church's Future," presentation at Elevate CSBC, 2017.

11. Will Mancini, *God Dreams: 12 Vision Templates for Finding and Focusing Your Church's Future* (Nashville: B&H Publishing Group, 2016), 46-48.

12. Aubrey Malphurs and Gordon E. Penfold, *Re:Vision, The Key to Transforming Your Church* (Grand Rapids: Baker Books, 2014), 147–51.

13. Ibid., 152.

Chapter 14

1. J. D. Payne, *Discovering Church Planting: An Introduction to the Whats, Whys, and Hows of Global Church Planting* (Colorado Springs: Paternoster, 2009), 143, emphasis original.

2. Mark Clifton, *Reclaiming Glory: Revitalizing Dying Churches* (Nashville: B&H Publishing Group, 2016), 67.

3. An excellent strategic plan was developed by Covenant Church in Winterville, North Carolina. Although this proposal is not connected to a revitalization effort, it demonstrates how a church goes through developing a strategic plan. It can be found at: http://www.connect2covenant.com/docs/vision 2020web.pdf.

Numerous good strategic plans can be found on the Web. Not all will be ones that will be in agreement with evangelical doctrine, but they demonstrate that churches of all theological walks need revitalization, and they give examples for how to lead a congregation into and through strategic planning.

4. Adapted from Payne, *Discovering Church Planting*, 156–57.

5. Aubrey Malphurs, *Advanced Strategic Planning: A New Model for Church and Ministry Leaders* (Grand Rapids: Baker Books, 1999), 165.

Chapter 15

1. Robert D. Dale, *To Dream Again: How to Help Your Church Come Alive* (Eugene, OR: Wipf and Stock Publishers, 2004), 76.

2. James Emery White, "Seven Characteristics of an Effective Church Structure," http://www.crosswalk.com/blogs/dr-james-emery-white/seven-characteristics-of-an-effective-church-structure.html.

3. Tony Morgan, "Next Level Teams: How Fast Growing Churches Are Mobilizing Their Staff," a research project from The Unstuck Group and Vanderbloemen Search Group (The Unstuck Group, 2017), 9.

Chapter 16

1. John P. Kotter and Lorne A. Whitehead, *Buy-In: Saving Your Good Idea from Getting Shot Down* (Boston: Harvard Business Review Press, 2010), 181.

2. Ibid., 6.

Conclusion

1. Thom S. Rainer, "Ten Symptoms of a Sick Church," http://www.lifeway.com/pastors/2017/06/13/ten-symptoms-sick-church/.

Appendices

1. See Pat MacMillan, *The Performance Factor* (Nashville: B&H, 2001).

2. The 12 Competencies were developed by Danny Rumple and others for the West Virginia Convention of Southern Baptists. Used by permission.

3. Charles Tidwell, *Church Administration: Effective Leadership for Ministry* (Nashville: B&H Publishing Group, 1985), 27.

Also Available by
BILL HENARD

Churches are closing today at an alarming rate. Pastors are disillusioned, church members are discouraged, and the world has lost interest. Can this disturbing tide be stemmed?

Bill Henard believes that there is hope for the established church – for your church. Some people may have already pronounced the church "dead," but these dead bones can live. Whether your church is seven years old or one-hundred and seventy, you may be seeing evidences that your church needs vision, direction, and revitalization.

Don't lose hope. Your church can live.